"If you want to unlock your [...] success in your life, *The Success Compass* will show you how to [...] at higher levels than ever before."

Brian Tracy, Author of *Flight Plan*

"You may have many books in your library but you won't find a more practical, relevant or systematic guide on how to manage your thinking and maximize your efforts."

"Coach" Lou Holtz, ESPN analyst, former Notre Dame Head Football Coach

"This book synthesizes some of the best principles in personal development and offers ageless wisdom in a fresh and contemporary format that is a must read for all success-oriented individuals."

Blair Singer, Author of *Sales Dogs, Little Voice Mastery*, and a Rich Dad Advisor

"No matter where you are on your journey to achievement, *The Success Compass* will serve as a solid guide to maximizing who you are and unlocking who you can become."

Bobby Bowden, Former Head Football Coach, Florida State University

"Kevin has hit a home run with the perspectives in *The Success Compass*. Regardless of where you want to succeed in life, whether it be in business, sales, athletics or anywhere in between, this book is a must read to help you bridge the gap from where you are to where you want to go."

Patrick Snow, International Best-Selling Author of *Creating Your Own Destiny*

"Anytime I can get help and understanding, I deem it worthwhile, especially when it is based on a great way of life. *The Success Compass* provides this with its organization and guidance in moving forward. As simple as it appears to be in content, it actually is quite intricate in meaning. I need it available when I need it …. often!"

Dan Gable, Iowa & USA Wrestling

"Author Kevin Hocker does an outstanding job of weaving Biblical teachings, the Law of Attraction, and every-day examples into this wise and witty book. With examples as diverse as Gilligan's Island to a Rocky movie, *The Success Compass* shares solid principles of life and success in a new and refreshing way. Highly recommended."

Lynne Klippel, Best-Selling Author of *Overcomers, Inc*

"With clarity and courage, Kevin offers inspiration to be the very best you can be. *The Success Compass* forces you to expand your horizons and reach for the stars. If you want to take a quantum leap in your personal development, then this book is an absolute "must read!"

Susan Friedmann, CSP, Author of
Riches in Niches: How to Make it BIG in a small Market

"To blaze new trails in your life you need to blaze new trails in your thinking! *The Success Compass* will give you the techniques, perspectives and encouragement to do just that."

Christine Kloser, Best Selling Author of *The Freedom Formula*

"Every principle in this book will impact your life with extraordinary results."

Kate Raidt, Author of *The Million-Dollar Parent*

"Quench your thirst with Kevin Hocker's no nonsense guidance toward true self-esteem and accomplishment. This book paves the road out of victim-mode to living boldly in faith based trust."

Julie Bookout Johnson, Author of *Creating Your Dream Team*

"*The Success Compass*" shows you how to control the controllable, manage the manageable and advance through adversity as you journey toward your goals."

Brad McColl, Author of *Leveraging Your Banker*

"From the title of this book, to the inspiring content you will be empowered by the principles that are with in."

Mary West, Co-Author of *YOUR ultimate SALES FORCE*

3/17/10

Carol,

It is a pleasure to know you. I wish you the best in all your endeavors.

I hope The Success Compass is a valuable tool for your journey.

Best,

Kevin Hocker

THE
SUCCESS
COMPASS

YOUR ROADMAP FOR RESULTS

A Powerful Guide For Setting Your Goals
A Clear Map For Reaching Them

━ KEVIN HOCKER ━

The Success Compass
Your Roadmap For Results

Address all inquiries to:
Kevin Hocker
6209 Mid Rivers Mall Dr, Suite 290
Saint Charles, MO 63304
Phone: 1-877-317-4167

www.TheSuccessCompass.com

ISBN 978-1-890427-19-1

Library of Congress Control Number: 2010900026

Editors: Beverly Holloran, Morgan Chilson and Jeannine Mallory
Cover Design & Interior Layout: www.fusioncw.com

Printed in the United States of America

For additional copies, visit: www.TheSuccessCompass.com

DEDICATION

To my wonderful wife, Cathy, who is the mother of our precious children, Madelynn and Dylan. While I consider this book a treasured accomplishment, it would mean nothing without the foundation of your love and support underneath it. You have sacrificed more than I could ever repay, and I am grateful for your encouragement, belief and faith in me. I Love You!

To my mom, Sharon Hocker: Mom, you are the model of unselfishness and servant-hood. Your dedication and sacrifice as a single parent provided more for Mike and me than many kids with two parents. I am forever grateful for the values you instilled in me and for exemplifying the attributes of love, character, integrity and kindness. You have long been the driving force for many of my goals and if I can do for you a fraction of what you have done for me then I have lived a good life. Thank you for everything. I love you.

To my only sibling: Mike Hocker. Mike, I can't imagine not having a brother and I certainly can't imagine not having you as my brother. Your ability to be honest with yourself and others is admirable. Your discipline, dedication and commitment to excellence are values I even find hard to live up to. You are an encouragement and the epitome of what a brother is all about. I love you bro!

ACKNOWLEDGMENTS

The completion of this book has more to do with others than it does with me. I will be forever grateful to those who first traveled the journey of self-discovery and in turn left immeasurable instructions for those of us who followed. It would require an additional book to acknowledge everyone who has had a positive impact on my life. However, there are certain people who have contributed in such a way that I am compelled to thank them.

Beyond my family are countless individuals who contributed to my growth and development. Some of them passed on before I was able to meet them, yet their wisdom shaped me in ways I could never repay. Thank you to the late Earl Nightingale, Og Mandino, Bill Bright, Fred Smith and Napoleon Hill. It is with sadness that I add Jim Rohn to this list as he passed during the final stages of my writing. Jim was an amazing contributor to my life and shaped my thinking like no one else.

My high school wrestling coach, Grodie Crick, was a much needed mentor. Thanks for your tough love and always believing in me. You brought out my best and encouraged me to get my act together by caring about not just Kevin the wrestler, but Kevin the person.

Dan Gable, thank you for inspiring me by the way you live your life and through your book (the first real book I ever read), *The Legend of Dan Gable, The Wrestler*. This book gave me a blueprint for how to be a champion on and off the mat and many opponents would have surely preferred that your book never made it to my hands. It also gave me the reassurance that a book can change someone's life and helped me to never doubt my own book project.

I, of course, must also thank Steve Noriega, an Indiana state wrestling champion, who inspired me to take wrestling very seriously and taught me who Dan Gable was.

I would like to thank some of my very best friends and spiritual mentors who have shaped my character, encouraged me, supported me and believed in me. Each one of you has a unique and special place in my heart: Rocky Prasse, Mike Liston, Jack Benninghoffen, Paul Dau, Todd Frisch, Jim Cunningham, C.R. Kersten, Wade Davis, Chris Frankenfield, Murphy Ownbey, Kevin Pyatt, Todd Lokey, Patrick Snow (my awesome coach), Jim Helbig, Jim Dunn, Matt Nicolls (thanks for everything Matt- you're a true Christian brother) Ben Douglas,

Bob Sander (who seems to "get" me better than most people) and everyone in my MenSharperners group.

A big thank you to my Pastor, Jeff Perry. You captivated me the first time I walked in to St Louis Family Church and Cathy and I have never looked back. You guided us through some tough valleys and helped us land on some incredible mountaintops. We've got your back and thanks for having ours.

I would like to extend a special thanks to Eric Freesmier. Eric, you have been a blessing in countless ways and been the wise counsel I needed many times. Thanks for all your support and encouragement as I completed this book. It has meant more than you could know.

There are also two incredible ladies who helped shape my business and personal philosophy. Thank you to Marie Madden and Susan Redmon. I am so blessed to have spent a brief season of my life under your wings. You are two of the most dynamic business women I have ever met and I will never forget you two!

I would like to thank David Fielder. We always said that eagles don't flock. And even though we have decided to travel down separate paths there will always be a part of you with me in all my journeys. For the longest time you believed in me more than I believed in myself. You saw what I was capable of when I didn't. Your encouragement and belief in me put me on a road I may have never found. I am forever grateful.

I would also like to acknowledge two of my best friends from my earlier years, Anthony Butts and Johnny Liggett. Both of you were part of my life in different seasons that left permanent and cherished experiences.

I must thank my personal development mentors who shared their brilliant thinking, helped me form much of my personal philosophy and equipped me with critical skills. There are too many of you to list but I could never leave out Brian Tracy, Blair Singer, Robert Kiyosaki, Jayne Johnson, Jack Canfield, T.Harv Eker, Mark Victor Hansen, Wayne Dyer, and the one and only, Lou Holtz. Years ago, Lou's book, *Winning Everyday*, lifted me out of one of the biggest pits of depression and discouragement I had ever faced. It was another reminder of how a book can be the biggest life preserver you can give someone.

I would also like to thank Bill Gouldd for raising my level of awareness in so many areas. It scares me to death to think where I would be if I had not had the privilege of learning from you.

Finally, I would like to thank my executive assistant, Beverly Holloran. Your support, dedication and loyalty are beyond what I could have ever hoped for. Thanks for everything, and especially your endless hours of editing to help bring forth this project.

CONTENTS

INTRODUCTION

*"We are drowning in information but
starved for knowledge."*
~ John Naisbitt

Our chaotic economy, fast-moving Information Age
and ever-changing society will transport many people down
the road of success. Unfortunately, it will transport even more
people down the road of failure. The difference between these
two extremes will not be about what happens, but rather what
you think (and do) about what happens.

Being conscious of what and how you think is more
important than ever before. Staying positive, optimistic, and
motivated does not happen automatically. It requires a constant
influx of new ideas, perspectives and a persistent cultivation of
mental toughness. And that is what the Success Compass is all
about.

As a lifelong student of the principles of success and achievement, I've accumulated a vast amount of information that can lead people to new heights in personal achievement. The principles will help you overcome fears, manage doubts and dust off those dreams you may have put on the shelf.

If you learn, embrace and apply these principles, you'll achieve great success in all your endeavors – and your life will be *forever changed* in a positive way. By making these principles part of your life, you'll be ensured a more productive career and you'll enjoy more fulfillment in the other areas of your life as well.

Let me say early on that I don't think of this as a Christian book. However, I am a Christian author. Through my years of study, I've discovered one theme: no matter how many books I've read or seminars I have attended, I have yet to find a success principle that I couldn't also find in the Bible. Many writers, including myself, have made considerable attempts to pass on the ultimate and timeless wisdom with fresh perspectives for the purpose of helping others.

I'm not a member of the clergy, nor do I have a degree in theology. I don't plan on sharing any moral or political convictions. I'm not here to tell you who or what to believe. I'm not going to profess that I'm right about everything or that I have all the answers. In fact, I run from teachers and books that proclaim to have "the" answer – no matter what the question!

I like what Nobel Prize Winner Andre Gide said: "Believe those who are seeking the truth; doubt those who find it."

I also realize that despite my best intentions, I run the risk of being misinterpreted, especially when offering perspectives that may back into someone's religious beliefs. Let me assure you that I am not proposing any definitive interpretation of the spiritual or scriptural points I make. In fact, some points are not meant to be taken 100% literally.

My ultimate purpose in writing this book is to share the most significant and meaningful principles I've learned to help you in your quest of reaching your full potential.

I'm not perfect; I make mistakes just like everybody does. At times I say things I shouldn't say, do things I shouldn't do and act in ways I shouldn't act. Despite those things, I refuse to allow guilt, shame or condemnation stop me from becoming all I can become.

Your Story is My Story

Even though we haven't met, I probably know a little about you. Maybe some of the points below apply to you?

- You expected to be further along in life than you are right now.

- Your shelves are filled with books and audio programs that were supposed to deliver the "hidden" secrets to wealth and success, the steps to achievement and the rules for personal growth.

- The complexity of the information age and the ever-changing and endless "expert advice" about how to achieve success has left you tired, overwhelmed, frustrated and confused.

- Every now and then you become resigned to the fact that life "is what it is." You accept what comes your way and rationalize it by declaring it could always be worse.

- Sometimes you find it's easier to hide, have a beer and forget about everything for a while.

Well, did I get close to describing at least some aspect of your life? I'm going to guess I did, because the life I described above is the way most people live today. But the good news is — it doesn't have to be that way. Stick with me and we'll change it all for the better!

The story of my quest for success began more than 18 years ago when I started working with a direct sales company. During that time, I met a man who proved to be one of my greatest mentors. With enthusiasm, I expressed my desire to succeed and he shared his ideas with me. His words, and what he taught me, inspired me. Many of his lessons focused on achieving wealth. Over time, I learned there's much more to life than money. I've modified what I learned and incorporated it into all areas of my life.

One of the first things he taught me was that if you want to be prosperous, then you should never take advice from people who don't have money. He also said that if you want to achieve what other people have achieved, then you must do what others have done. He told me that if I wanted things to improve, then *I* had to improve. He went on to say things like... for things to get better, *I* had to get better, for my bank account to grow, *I* had to grow and if *I* wanted things to change, then *I* had to change.

He motivated me to continually seek new ideas and inspiration. I began to read personal development books, attend motivational seminars and listen to educational tapes in my car. I set forth on a personal development quest and never looked back.

Since then, my life has been an upward, unbroken path of constant improvement – and things keep getting better. Sure, I've had some failures and losses along the way. But I've had many wins and successes. It's both the wins *and* the losses that help us achieve what we most want in life. I've lost money on several business ventures, but what I learned from those experiences allowed me to pick up the pieces and organize companies that produced more than a million dollars' revenue within the first year, and I've done it more than once.

In fact, I owe many of my greatest accomplishments to failure.

"Life is a grindstone, and whether it grinds one man down or polishes him up depends on what he is made of."
~ Josh Billings (Henry Wheeler Shaw)

In this book I will refer to the Law of Attraction several times, but you'll discover this is *not* just a book about the Law of Attraction. It's a book describing the most relevant, important and timeless principles you can use to achieve success… and the Law of Attraction just happens to be one of the more important principles to do that. I'll address quite a few points about the Law of Attraction in the early parts of the book and then reference it other places as we move along.

If you're new to this theory, then you're probably wondering what this "Law of Attraction" is; or maybe even wondering if you've broken it! If you've never heard about any of this before, be prepared now because you'll start hearing about it everywhere. That alone will demonstrate one of its most valid aspects.

If the Law of Attraction is new to you, it may sound mysterious and you may be reluctant to proceed with this book. Let me assure you: what people call the "Law of Attraction" is a fancy way of re-packaging and teaching what God created in the first place.

The concept behind the Law of Attraction is that **you are like a magnet**. Therefore, you attract into your life that which is in harmony with your thinking. This includes, but is not limited to, your home, your car, your relationships, your career and your finances. If you believe "you become who you hang around with" or "birds of a feather flock together," then you should also believe in the Law of Attraction. It's the same as we read in Proverbs: "As a man thinketh in his heart, so is he."

In my opinion, some marketers and New Age teachers have exploited the concept and taken it down some very interesting roads. I believe what Scripture says and that's why I want to clean up some loose ends and misconceptions in the first couple of chapters of this book. I feel it's necessary when relating to this topic.

Additionally, you're going to notice I interchange words such as spirit, universe, the Law of Attraction and God. This is not to tell you how or what to label things. The principles in this book are rock solid. If you're not so sure about the way I incorporate these or any other words, please substitute words that resonate with *you*.

Before we go further, let me explain why the principles that follow, many of which you already know, might work more effectively after you've finished this book. Whether you decide to adopt all the ideas set forth here, some of them or none of them at all, I believe the fundamental ingredient for achieving success is to have a system in place for every area of your life.

In the case of **The Success Compass,** I'm talking about a **thinking system**.

A Thinking System

Begin to think about things that function with great efficiency and effectiveness – cars, computers, airplanes or the human body, just to name a few. These things function properly because something else functions properly. The "something else" is the system behind them.

For example, let's say you're driving and your alternator gives out. Your car stops dead in its tracks. What really happened? Did the entire car "break down," or did one specific component of the *system* that sustains the car break down?

Let's take another example. What happens when someone has the flu? Did the person just get sick? Or did a weakness in the person's immune *system* allow a virus or bacteria to survive and multiply, which, in turn, caused the fever, cough and body aches we associate with the flu?

My point is this, if something works well, then it has a good system behind it. If something works on an average level, then it has an average system behind it. If something doesn't work well, then there's either a malfunction in the system or – even worse – *no system at all*.

So when it comes to something as in-depth as personal growth and the application of success principles, don't you think it would make sense – and be necessary – to have a system in place for those major processes too? That's what I'm providing here in *The Success Compass*. There are hundreds of good books on the market about success and achievement. There are also many excellent teachers, websites and seminars. These sources are invaluable and I've obtained much of my education this way.

The problem for me has always been the sheer *volume* of information out there. It's overwhelming! What makes my book unique is that I've condensed some of the best principles ever discovered and then provided an easy-to use thinking system to apply them. See, some of the books and seminars I learned from provided so much information I didn't even know where to start. I found myself piling up notebook after notebook – and leaving many ideas on the shelf.

Finally, I realized the ideas and information weren't the problem. The problem was not having a "mental" system to organize and apply what I learned. The lack of a system caused my self-study and application to break down on the road to discovery… that is until I created a simple system.

Set Your Goals with the "*Success Compass*"

Let me give you a visual to help you better understand the importance of my system, the **Success Compass**, which I'll outline in Part two. Because there are certain steps to any system, let's use a drive-thru car wash as a metaphor. The car wash begins when you pay and enter your code on the key pad and ends when your car goes through the drying process. All the cycles between (the pre-soak, undercoating, wash, rinse, dry, etc.) are what you go through to achieve the final destination.

Now, what if you skipped the soak cycle in a car wash and just went directly to the soap? Would that produce the best results? What if you put Armor All® on the tires first and then went through the wash cycle? Obviously, the soap would wash away most of the Armor All® and leave few, if any, results.

Having a system takes the guesswork out of a multitude of details and systematically helps you decide what you need to know and when you need to know it. It helps you decide what you need to do and when you need to do it. It allows you to make decisions, prioritize plans and execute ideas in an accumulating, steady and logical order. Having a system gives you freedom to be more confident and relaxed, and you are less likely to get sidetracked or make mistakes.

My goal in creating the *Success Compass* was to provide a simple concept for thinking about (and, of course, attaining) your goals in a more effective way. The *Success Compass* helps you organize and maximize everything you've learned (and will continue to learn) in your ongoing personal development journey. All the quotes, philosophies, strategies and ideas remain in your subconscious mind and rise to the occasion as you need them while you execute this simple formula.

The Success Compass

Here's a quick snapshot of the Success Compass. There are only three components to it, and I will explain each one in much greater detail in Part Two of this book. In part, you'll find this is similar to using a GPS or other navigation system:

> **Program:** First, you need to know where you're going – your destination. Once you have that information, then insert it (i.e. program it/write it down) into the GPS of your mind and spirit. Don't worry about making your destination extremely precise, at least not at first. You should, however, have a general idea of where you want to go before you start your journey. I think people have been told they must know *exactly* where they want to go in order to achieve their goals, or for the Law of Attraction to work or to activate the subconscious mind. Sure, doing that may be more effective and quicker, but too many people end up doing nothing because they don't know

exactly where they want to go. Let's put an end to that right now.

Drive: Now, get moving! Even if you make a few false starts or need to turn around and start over, any movement is better than sitting still! German philosopher Meister Johannes Eckhart summed it up when he said, "The price of inaction is far greater than the cost of making a mistake." If you want to achieve your goals, you must begin moving toward them. Once you've programmed your GPS, the route to get you there will unfold if you keep your eyes open.

Arrive: You *will* get there. It might not be the destination you envisioned. You could end up somewhere you never imagined, maybe earning less (or more) than you expected. You may not always arrive exactly at the location you programmed, and most times it's for the best. In his inspiring and unforgettable song, "Unanswered Prayers," Garth Brooks reminded us that some of the greatest gifts we receive can be in the form of unanswered prayers. Besides, every arrival is an opportunity to program a new destination!

It's that simple. The Success Compass will become the system behind your thought process. It will, in short, become your *new* thinking system. With the Success Compass, not only will your journey become a lot shorter and simpler, it will become a lot more rewarding!

"The Promised Land always lies on the other side of a Wilderness."
~Havelock Ellis

This book was written for those who desire to live in the present while simultaneously working to create their future. It is for those who desire to become the very best they are capable of becoming. It is for people who demand the best of themselves and set high standards to live by. It is for those of you who know that the responsibility of controlling your thoughts is an extremely tough and ongoing battle, but it is a battle you are committed to winning. It is for those of you who will never stop learning and will keep fighting until you reach all the dreams and goals you set out to accomplish.

In short, this book is for tough people who are committed to going through tough stuff to get where they want to go. And that is also why it stands on the Christian principles I believe in. There were some pretty tough people in the Bible. People who sacrificed, worked hard, endured harsh conditions, overcame obstacles, experienced fear, doubt, betrayal and dealt with torture and agonizing deaths to stand up for what they believe in. Are you willing to do all that?

The only place I know where to find mentors that BIG is in a little book. And while everyone will benefit, I feel Christians will gain even more because they will learn how to more effectively use this law, which has often been improperly presented as something "mystical."

The Law of Attraction is as godly as the sky is blue as long as your trust is not in the law itself, but rather in the One who created the law. No matter what you personally want to call it, God makes it clear through His word that once you shape and organize your thinking, your thinking will shape and organize you.

This book is broken into two sections, each complete in its own way. It's kind of like needing to learn the alphabet before you can read and write.

Part One covers many of the foundational success principles necessary for achievement in any area of life. By mastering these, you will naturally experience the "coincidences" many call the Law of Attraction.

Part Two consists of the *Success Compass* system. It will help maximize your cooperation with all success principles, including the Law of Attraction, and give you a simple system in which to maximize the toughest job on earth, controlling your thoughts, as you embark on the journey toward your goals.

Finally, it's my hope that every chapter in *The Success Compass* will cause you to feel complete and whole as you begin to give your thoughts to the world and, at last, have the world give you your thoughts.

PART

1

GETTING READY
FOR THE TRIP

1

I THINK WE TOOK A WRONG TURN

"If you think education is expensive, try ignorance."
~ **Derek Bok**

Many teachers and writers today focus on the Law of Attraction. Diligent students jump from book to book and teacher to teacher in hopes of finding the mental equivalent of the Holy Grail. Why another book about success? Why another book that addresses the Law of Attraction?

And why *now*?

With its promises of effortless success and profound results, many are eager to study the Law of Attraction. These extraordinary concepts and promises cause students to immerse themselves in the philosophy, hoping to master its principles. Often, and despite the purest motives, these students lose sight of reality as they strive to become their own miracle workers.

As a result, individuals who started out enthusiastic and hopeful about achieving their dreams often become confused and discouraged as they watch their thoughts fail to become "things." Despite their discouragement, however, many continue on with the belief that the Law of Attraction works and they are just not good at it yet. This persistent denial of reality leaves them exposed, lost and usually more confused than when they began.

Too many students of the Law of Attraction fall prey to a purportedly "easy" way to achieve success. As known today, the Law of Attraction has many teachers with many perspectives. All of them offer valuable and sometimes life-changing insight. However, very few of them have built, filtered or completed their analysis with a Christian viewpoint. Some may pick and choose a scripture to support a specific idea, but few go beyond that.

This New Age version of the Law of Attraction wants us to believe that we can control the wind and the waves. I believe the Law of Attraction isn't about controlling the wind and the waves – it's about controlling the set of the sail. As the late Jim Rohn (an amazing motivator and business philosopher) always taught his students.

Ironically, if we learn to better manage what *we can* control, then our lives will unfold with the majestic appearance that we do control the wind and the waves. The logical question then becomes: would it be better to sail in the ocean of life and spend most of our time trying different techniques to get the wind and waves to obey (something we *can't control*) or spend our time improving how we set the sail (something we *can control*)? Let me say from experience that trying to control the world is hard work.

While many books and courses teach these timeless principles, I believe the core of understanding, especially as it relates to the Law of Attraction, must include insight into what God says about the matter. I'm not here to preach, witness, condemn or judge. Nor am I here to push my Christian beliefs on you. I **am** here, however, to help you reach your destination. I will do so in the best way I know. More importantly, I will teach you a method that ***works***.

The **Success Compass** will provide a guide that will lead you to prosperity and success in *every* area of your life. But it also serves another purpose. In your quest for success, you've undoubtedly yearned and searched for the best ideas. You've read books, tried this philosophy, applied that quote and you've never stopped looking for the magic bullet. Yet despite everything you've seen, heard or read, maybe you're still asking, "Is there one source, a sound philosophy, a reliable path or a universal law I can apply to acquire the future I'm looking for?"

I asked all those questions and searched for these things for a long time. I found some very good answers, and they worked temporarily; but like a new car, they lost their luster and "new car" appeal after a while.

That finally changed when I learned to improve the focus of my personal development efforts. The richest and wisest man who ever lived said, "How much better to get wisdom than gold! And to get understanding is to be chosen rather than silver."

I think those words are some of the best advice we could ever get. But what kind of wisdom should we seek? I believe the most important wisdom we can obtain falls in two areas: 1) Knowledge of the timeless principles, all which can be found in books, and of course in the Bible and; 2) Knowledge of how our minds work. If we focus on these two areas, and blend them with other success principles, then we can not only build anything we want, but we'll also know how.

The Success Compass may just be the most important book you read as it relates to success principles and the Law of Attraction. I know it's a bold statement, but I make it with confidence because this unique book is built *on* Christian principles, not next to them. Another reason I feel confident you'll benefit greatly is because this book has less to do with what I teach you and more to do with what I hope to inspire you to learn. Albert Einstein said, "I never teach my pupils. I only attempt to provide the conditions in which they can learn." I have the same objective here. Much of what you will learn will come indirectly as you ponder new philosophies and raise your awareness.

While it's certainly my goal to teach you, I ultimately hope to inspire you to reach for new levels in teaching yourself.

Sure, there may be better books about the Law of Attraction, achieving success and being a Christian, but you won't find one that blends the topics as you'll see here. Because of this and the simplicity of the book, I believe you'll make incredible progress in your thinking and, subsequently, every other area of your life also.

Long gone is the Industrial Age and, for better or worse, the Information Age is here to stay. It is a time of far less farming and far more filing; way too many meetings and far too little movement. And the majority of our daily stress is more related to our ability to cope with circumstances rather than the circumstances themselves.

"External" advancements in technology were supposed to make life easier, but most people still think the way they always have: three meals a day, with nine-to-five business hours and a gold watch at the end. We're using eight-track mindsets in an iPod world.

Despite current economic conditions, people are prospering more than ever. However, you'll rarely get an update about it on the six o'clock news or see an inspiring article on the front page of the newspaper.

I was driving down the highway several months ago and noticed a new building under construction. I didn't know what it was, but each week I saw a little more progress with the construction project. Then, finally, I saw a sign go up: *Lamborghini*.

My initial thought was, "You've got to be kidding! A Lamborghini dealership? Who in the world could be in the market for a Lamborghini? And more so, who would be crazy enough to think this is a good time to build a Lamborghini dealership? Businesses all around here have closed their doors." As I pondered this, I let it work for me instead of against me.

The tough economic times many are experiencing are actually an exciting period for a lot of people. The difference in my opinion is very simple. *You see what you look at*. And, if you look at history, you'll find amazing statistics and surprises that should give you hope about the future, not distress.

Think about it for a minute: according to the media, from an economic standpoint, it's as though we are in the second Great Depression (or Depression 2.0, as it's now being called). While I didn't live through the Great Depression, I do know what came after it.

In that time, many people thought the world as they knew it was over. Now, think about our current society. Just walk through a mall, an electronics store or drive a late model car. We have laptops, software, GPS, the world wide web, email, cell phones, space shuttles, digital cameras, iPods, text messaging, wireless headsets, Bluetooth technology, Blackberries, iPhones, microwaves, HDTV, DirecTV, YouTube and the newest Lexus can parallel park itself. I could go on, but if this is the kind of stuff produced *after* an economic hardship, then we might just want to hang on to the words in 1 Thessalonians 5:18 and "give thanks in all circumstances." In fact, I would like to pause for a moment of silence and thank God for Tivo and that VHS tapes are a thing of the past!

Happy, sad, good times, bad times, pretty, ugly, rich or poor – **<u>it's all in your mind</u>**. When asked about the next ten years, one of my favorite teachers and mentors, Jim Rohn, says, "It will probably be pretty much like the last ten. We will have opportunity mixed with adversity and adversity mixed with opportunity." Good advice!

There are now more millionaires than ever and it doesn't have nearly as much to do with the value of the dollar. It's because more people are increasing their knowledge, their skills, and they are learning to use their minds more effectively. The media can often cause you to believe otherwise, but what you accept makes all the difference. Your mind has brought you to where you are and your mind will take you where you're going. Let's just make sure you're not a backseat driver.

I love the way John Milton put it: "The mind is its own place. And in itself can make a heaven of Hell, and a hell of Heaven."

Where is Your Personal Crossroads?

As we journey through these pages, I don't know where you are in life and your own personal quest for success and prosperity. Maybe life is going great. Maybe life *was* going great, but now you're in a crisis. Or maybe life has always been "just okay," and you're tired of "okay."

Well, what about you? Yes, you, the one who's frustrated, tired and maybe even angry. You've put in a lot of hard work, created opportunities for yourself, made your thought life a priority and still, "just okay" is all you can muster.

In fact, you're beginning to doubt you can create the life you want. You use to believe you could; it made sense. Do ABC and you'll get XYZ. Isn't that what the Law of Attraction promises? And still you persist. You haven't given up completely. That's why you are holding another book, hoping it will contain the advice, mindset or strategy to take you to the life you know is possible if you can just figure things out. You hope this book will hold some of the missing links, perspectives and the keys you have yet to find.

Well, I think it will.

Are you a Christian, a believer in the Law of Attraction — or both? Are you a student of personal development? Do you sometimes struggle with creating what you want and wonder what you're doing to cause the disconnection between what you think and what you receive?

Have you lost some of your hope and passion because you can't seem to break through and rise out of the confusion? Have you seen the Law of Attraction succeed enough not to doubt it, but seen it fail enough not to trust it?

If you feel this way, then you are holding the right book at the right time. I know where you're coming from because **I have been there myself**. Before I give you any additional advice or instructions, I am going to say this: RELAX.

Remember, the intelligence that created you holds this entire universe together. It placed the earth at just the right distance from the sun and has more systems in place than we will ever understand. It keeps you breathing while you are asleep; it causes your heart to beat and pumps your blood. It knows everything you want to do, be and have. It also knows everything required to bring it all about. Therefore, everything that happens has been perfectly orchestrated to assist you, even if sometimes it hurts like heck.

The Law of Attraction is a mainstream topic today and there are many good teachers and books on the subject. I have learned a tremendous amount from many of them and credit a significant amount of my own growth to the perspectives they offered.

And yet, in all the books I've read and benefited from, there was always something… *missing*. I don't think it was necessarily something authors unknowingly left out, but rather I think it was something they simply didn't acknowledge. And that's okay, because I'm going to.

In fact, I believe many teachers steer clear of some important distinctions in discussing the Law of Attraction. Because of this I think a few students end up with significant frustration and incorrect perceptions, despite all the good they do learn. For them, like me, there was always something missing.

It's time to fill the gaps, connect the dots and include the missing links.

The Law of Attraction's Missing Links

If it's ok I would like to take a quick timeout. I want to make a couple of disclosures before I lose any of you.

First, I am not going to be thumping you in the head with a Bible throughout this book. In making a few points here at the beginning I will use several scriptures to support my point. And I am doing this for you, not me. I don't want you to take my word for anything. I want you to come to your own conclusion. That's how transformation is made.

If you are thinking this book is going to be a Sunday school class on steroids, you've got another thing coming. If you have any doubt, then please skip to Chapter 2.

Second, this book is not about how to incorporate the missing links I am about to share. Rather, it is more about how to think and live once they are incorporated. I am going to put a few key points on the table that just might make the difference for you. You can take them or leave them. From there we are going to move on and talk about how to achieve the goals you want to accomplish.

Now, let's get back to it.

What makes this book different from other books you've read? Well, besides the unique perspectives and transformational examples, I am also going to lay the foundation of this book on some of the topics that are rarely included in the many books about personal development and/or the Law of Attraction.

And this is not just my idea. Jesus even shared an analogy about it to make a critical point. He says, "Therefore everyone who hears these words and puts them into practice is like a wise man who built his house on the rock." He wraps up his story by explaining that everyone who hears His words and *does not* put them into practice is like a foolish man who built his house on sand.

I Once Was Found, *but* Now I'm Lost

If anyone has messed up the above instructions, it's me. In the past I'd become such a diligent student of the Law of Attraction that I started to ignore what I knew as Christian truth. I began to crave the easy philosophy that said I could create anything if only I learned how to manage my "vibrations." Well, the Bible mentions a lot of things, but it never once mentions the word vibration.

I disregarded all three of the missing links I am going to talk about. But our Creator had us figured out before the beginning of time. That is why we have the following admonishments:

If anyone comes to you and does not bring this teaching, do not take him into your house or welcome him. We are told to hold firmly to the trustworthy message as it has been taught and to stand firm and hold to the teachings passed on to us. We are also warned of false teachers who promote myths and endless genealogies.

And if that isn't enough, we also learn that *the day will come when men will not put up with sound doctrine. Instead, to suit their own desires they will gather around them a great number of teachers to say what their itching ears want to hear. They will turn their ears away from the truth and turn aside to myths.*

And finally, in what I think is one of the biggest challenges in the Law of Attraction teachings, is what God himself revealed early on in the instruction book; "*Do not add to what I command you and do not subtract from it, but keep the commands of the Lord your God that I give you.*"

So what's my point? In this age of many voices, religions, teachers and authors, it's easy for people to get caught up in a style of thinking or a particular philosophy that resonates with them and promises ease. I think that's what happens to many students and even well-meaning Christians. They have good intentions, but they become swayed by the promises of teachers who leave out, in my opinion, very important instructions.

For instance, most discussions of the Law of Attraction do not account for or acknowledge evil. You will also have a hard time finding the word "Satan" in a New Age book about the Law of Attraction. Yet we read: "For our struggle is not against flesh and blood, but against the rulers, against the authorities, against the powers of this dark world and against the spiritual forces of evil in the heavenly realms." A few verses later we are told to take up the shield of faith, with which we can extinguish all the flaming arrows of the evil one.

We also receive important instructions about how to pray and yet within those instructions we learn it must be of critical importance to acknowledge evil because the prayer concludes with… "Deliver us from the evil one."

As I have indicated, I was kind of lukewarm in some areas. I was always quick to claim that with God all things are possible or that Jesus came to give abundant life. But I was only acknowledging the things I *wanted* to hear. The Law of Attraction became addicting because all I had to do to create my life was think it into existence, or so I thought.

Now, I don't know about you, but to be taught "I have come to give abundant life" without being taught "the thief comes to kill, steal and destroy" (John 10:10) would be like putting me in a football game without a helmet and shoulder pads.

New Age Law of Attraction states that we make our own lives by what we think (which is mostly true). But trying to apply the principles of Law of Attraction without acknowledging evil in the world can cause major stress. You'll fall prone to confusion, guilt, blame and all kinds of misinterpretations of events and circumstances. You may just drive yourself crazy; I almost did.

This is a mistake. Evil exists and if you have any doubt, just watch the news tonight. You'll need five minutes – no – five seconds, to see the evil in our world. Why deny this undisputable fact? We have night, day, male, female and we have good and evil. But how can we triumph if we don't know the rules, or even the participants, in this battle?

I think another significant area the Law of Attraction overlooks is how sin plays a role in our life and circumstances. Many students gladly sidestep this topic and immerse themselves in the New Age Law of Attraction because its teachers also sidestep the issue of sin. The choice is yours when it comes to this issue, but the Bible clearly states we will make mistakes (sin) and God will forgive us. However, if we never admit, acknowledge or attempt to reconcile our substandard behavior, then God will be on a mission to draw us to Him… and He does this out of His Love.

When we try applying Law of Attraction principles to create one thing while God is working on another, He will attempt to put us on the right path. We certainly have free will and I am not here to condemn a sinful lifestyle or make judgments about right or wrong. I am, however, trying to make it clear that if we try to run our lives contrary to what God wants for us, then He tends to step in!

In fact, listen to this: "My son, do not make light of the Lord's discipline, and do not lose heart when He rebukes you, because the Lord disciplines those He loves, and He punishes everyone He accepts as a son. Endure hardship as discipline; God is treating you as sons. For what son is not disciplined by his father?" That seems to make sense to me.

Now, consider the Law of Attraction student who is actually being dealt with by God out of love but thinks it is because they are using the Law of Attraction "wrong." Do you think this may cause frustration and confusion?

Another missing link involves action – a topic that has stirred up its fair share of debate. However, if we continue to draw on the foundational Source of Wisdom, we can glean real truth on the matter. We are told that "Faith without works is dead" and that a man reaps what he sows.

In Proverbs, we find several references to hammer home the point that action is necessary. Here is advice passed down from the wisest man who ever lived.

"He who works his land will have abundant food, but he who chases fantasies will have his fill of poverty."

"All hard work brings a profit, but mere talk leads only to poverty."

"I went past the field of the sluggard, past the vineyard of the man who lacks judgment; thorns had come up everywhere; the ground was covered with weeds and the stone wall was in ruins. I applied my heart to what I observed and learned a lesson from what I saw. A little sleep, a little slumber, a little folding of the hands to rest, and poverty will come on you like a bandit and scarcity like an armed man."

Critics of the Law of Attraction admonish the idea that you can "will" anything into your life without taking action or having to deal with any adversity. This type of philosophy is easy to sell but hard to buy. It sounds exciting and is exhilarating at first, but I believe it delivers the exact opposite of what it claims. Instead of setting people free, it actually traps them. It traps them in a faulty philosophy, which if persisted in, can cause more pain than it ever relieves.

How can you sit in your living room and "attract" a new car, a spouse, a new house, new job or a new life? But there's more to the Law of Attraction than wishing or willing things into existence. The Law says how we think, both consciously and unconsciously, dictates the reality of our lives – for better or worse. And for the most part that is true. Negative thoughts attract negative consequences, while positive thoughts attract positive consequences. Unfortunately, this is where most people stop; at least most teachers on the topic of the Law of Attraction.

Thought without action is merely imagination. Walt Disney was a dreamer, but he was also a doer. He knew that to attract the life he wanted, he needed to commit to a series of actions that helped him attract the very life he envisioned.

As the Russian proverb says, "Pray to God, but row for shore."

Would You Drive a Car With No Safety Features?

Please don't get the wrong idea; it is not my intent to criticize any other books or teachers. I have learned something positive from every teacher, and if I didn't first learn from their point of view I couldn't have offered the one I am giving you. Furthermore, I feel the student has an equal responsibility to continually seek answers, and not every teacher has them all. So, I'm simply trying to point out how *my* book is different and help you find what you just might be looking for.

Maybe you've struggled with a blended philosophy. Maybe you're ready to change. Ignoring evil, sin, action or any other timeless principle must result in a consequence. Evil, sin and action are realities of modern life; they were realities in the beginning of time, and they will remain realities as long as you and I are breathing. I think the light bulb went off for me when I realized that the Law of Attraction was not about me working through God, but God working through me.

Let me ask you this: Would you drive a car with no safety features? Well, that's what it's like when you read a book on the

Law of Attraction, success or personal development that suggests (directly or indirectly) that the missing links I've introduced are irrelevant. It sends you careening through life, expecting nothing but green lights, empty four-lane highways, premium parking spaces and a gumball machine on the dashboard!

But, metaphorically speaking, what happens when you get stuck in a traffic jam? What happens when someone rear-ends your car? What does it mean when all the good parking spots are taken or when you get a flat tire? In short, not factoring in evil, sin and action leaves you unprepared for the often harsh and always certain realities of day-to-day life in our hectic modern world.

Now is not the time to give up hope! You can still attract the life of your dreams. And by incorporating the "links," you'll be more prepared to send out into the world the right messages at the right time for the right reasons. This book will provide the safety features you need to enter the fast lane of your dreams. The blinders are finally off and the future looks bright!

> *Have you seen the Law of Attraction succeed enough not to doubt it, but seen it fail enough not to trust it?*

Review

- We need to be better at managing what we can control, not what we can't.

- We can't control the wind and the waves, only the set of the sail.

- You see what you look at...and you control where you look.

- The same intelligence that created you can surely take care of you.

- A chain is only as strong as its weakest link. The Law of Attraction is only as weak as its missing link.

2

CAN I SEE *YOUR* LICENSE & REGISTRATION PLEASE?

*"Always be a first-rate version of yourself,
instead of a second-rate version of
somebody else."*
~ Judy Garland

Once upon a time, our grandparents ran errands without locking the front door and, if they were in a hurry, even left the keys in the ignition while they popped into this store or that to pick up milk or bread. Unfortunately, those days are long gone.

Today we live in a world of securities fraud, investment scams and, of course, something our grandparents never even heard of: **identity theft**. Use your credit card online and there's a chance you could have thousands of dollars in unapproved charges on your next bill. Once stolen, it can take weeks, months or years to get your identity – and peace of mind – back.

People work hard to establish and maintain a good credit rating and protect their identities. Many even use commercial services that monitor suspicious activity to help spot identify theft. Despite their best efforts, it has been easy for thieves to steal Social Security numbers, bank account info, or credit card numbers.

Beyond this, there's another type of identity theft. It is sometimes stolen by others, but never without our permission. In these instances we fall prey to a problem much worse than a maxed-out credit card or a low credit score. Loss of this identity can leave us depressed, unmotivated, hopeless or filled with despair. The identity I'm talking about here is our self-esteem and self-image – our real identity.

In addition to everything we do to be cautious in our external world, the most extreme caution must be exercised against the biggest identity thief of all: our own self-doubt, the little voice in our heads and the opinions of others. We must also protect ourselves from the evil thief I mentioned earlier. It's the thief that most people ignore, the thief that attacks you where it is most effective… in your thoughts about yourself.

Every time we give into self-doubt, insecurity, fear or even paranoia based on lies or what modern life tells us we should or shouldn't do, we chip away a little bit more of our identity. Stop identity theft today. Deny those voices of doubt and derision and take back your self-esteem. It's the **only** way to allow the Law of Attraction to act in your life in any real and authentic way.

There is one teacher who has been particularly effective at raising my awareness, increasing my skills and shaping my thinking in a positive way and it is Brian Tracy. I started listening to Brian's programs with the intention of gaining sales skills. The first two programs I invested in were the *Psychology of Selling* (audio) and *Advanced Selling Strategies* (book, audio and coaching). I feel these programs are as important for a sales professional as oxygen is for the lungs. I purchased Brian's programs with the goal of becoming a better salesperson. I was looking for some good closing techniques and wanted to get better at overcoming objections. I also wanted to make more money!

Well, I got those things out of the programs, but not in the way I expected. When I began learning from Brian, I had no idea how much my limiting beliefs about myself were holding me back in life. I had no idea that my self-image and self-esteem were so critical to my success. Brian taught me that the only way I was going to achieve the external success I desired was to first develop a self-image that corresponded with it.

I owe much of my success to what I learned from Brian Tracy, but the real win for me wasn't just financial. Instead, the *real* win was the change in my self-esteem, self-respect and self-image. The turning point in my life wasn't a closing technique or a strategy for overcoming an objection; **it was learning to see myself differently on the inside.** Once I understood the importance of a positive self-image and began to upgrade how I saw myself, all the circumstances in my life began to upgrade as well.

I was always looking for a short cut and I found it through Brian. The fastest way to improve any area of your life is to improve how you think and feel about yourself. When you begin to see yourself differently you will begin to act and behave differently. And when you begin to act and behave differently, guess what? You will get different results.

If you build a house you must first lay the foundation, we all know that. However, if you want your house to *last*, you must not build that foundation on sand. Knowing and consciously applying the techniques to improve your cooperation with the Law of Attraction will be seriously limited if you don't also change the way you think about yourself.

Understanding who you are is the foundation upon which you build the image of yourself. Otherwise, it's like trying to put the roof on a house before you've pulled the permit, designed the blueprints, laid the concrete foundation or built the walls. I also mention "improving your cooperation with the Law of

Attraction" because you are not actually *learning* how to put the Law of Attraction in place.

The Law of Attraction is already in place; always has been and always will be. The good news (and bad) is that people will never be more than the way they see themselves. In other words, your life will always look like – and never go much further above or below – the picture and belief you have of yourself *on the inside*.

I was recently reminded of this principle in a rather humorous fashion. A friend of mine had some recordings of the original Gilligan's Island TV shows. If you are too young to remember, it was about a group of people who become shipwrecked on a deserted island. The entire show is a comical adventure of attempts to survive and ultimately escape their unfortunate fate. Anyway, after watching an episode for about 15 minutes I was struck with something I never would have noticed when I was younger. As the castaways begin reluctantly settling in on the island, something very interesting happens. They all begin to assume the role, the personality and the self-image they had of themselves "off" of the island. Each character becomes (on the island) who they see themselves (off the island). Two of the most interesting characters are the Howells. They are the condescending millionaires with a good dose of pretentiousness. The fact that their money is worthless on a deserted island does not stop them from "being" rich. They act, walk, talk and, of course, treat everybody like they always have. They expect better accommodations, better treatment, etc. The Howells knew who they were before they were shipwrecked and no circumstances were going to change that image. Ironically, because they saw themselves this way, so did everybody else. You are probably getting my point by now, but don't just look at this as a funny example. As I reflected on this story, I realized how much truth is in it. On one hand, the human psychology is very powerful and this is really good news. The problem, though, is too many people are shipwrecked on an island of doubt, fear, insecurity or mediocrity. They have landed on their own deserted island and assumed their identity. It is my hope that *The Success Compass* can rescue as many castaways as possible.

We've all known people who are "going to lose those last 20 pounds" or "going back to school and finish up my master's" or "going to be a big star," yet every time we see them in the grocery store – I'm talking through the years – they haven't lost any weight, haven't even picked up a college catalog, haven't gone on one audition. Self-belief is as limiting as it is liberating. The picture you create for yourself on the inside *does* affect how your life plays out on the outside, for better or worse.

Now, let's be clear, you don't work on and upgrade this inside picture (which has so much to do with your self-esteem) to support your foundation; you work on your foundation so it supports you. Whether or not someone likes you is up to that person; whether or not you like yourself is up to **you**.

These are examples to show how many of us have mixed up our priorities. We seek the outer before the inner; we ask before we answer or, for that matter, even search for the answer. **Chapter 2** is about putting the cart back behind the horse, where it belongs, and learning to put ourselves – or at least, how we think and feel about ourselves – first for a change.

Revise the Blueprints of Your Inner Foundation

The idea that our inside (mental) world affects our outside (physical) lives is nothing new. In fact, I will mention it so many times that you will probably say, "Okay, I get it!" I hope you do. I'll admit; I didn't get it at first. Even though I knew the basic principle, it wasn't easy for me to apply. I know that putting a little white ball in a hole is a pretty simple concept too, but it ain't always that easy to do!

I think part of the problem is that many people never really establish a good method or system that works for them when it comes to affecting and improving their inside world. We have thousands of self-help books, mentors, audio programs and gurus to choose from, but what might inspire and motivate one person may grate on someone else's nerves. Still, good books and seminars are great ways to improve your inside world and raise your awareness.

What I want to do in this chapter is give you some ideas, skills and perspectives to help you find what works best for you as a way to improve your inside world. I won't necessarily give these to you directly. It's my belief that by the time you finish this chapter, you will indirectly or subconsciously gain new and better methods for improving, strengthening and winning the battle in your inside world. "How," you may ask? Keep reading and find out!

Since we'll be working on the inside world, we need to understand what this inside world is made of. We need to examine the blueprints before we just grab a hammer and nails and take off to the job site.

As we will discover, the blueprints of your inner world consist of many components and, naturally, your words, thoughts, moods, attitudes and emotions make up a big part of how you view yourself. But in my opinion, the biggest part of your inside world is made up of a single picture. While your inside world contains many sub-images, the most important one is the picture and image you have of yourself.

Therefore, it is your image of self, i.e. your self-image that you need to upgrade, change or modify. Teachers approach improving self-image from many angles and most of them are good. What I've found is most of them base their teaching on a foundation that is bound to fail from time to time. And that foundation is, **us.**

You see, when we try to improve our self-image based **solely** on who we are, we naturally set ourselves up for disappointment. Yes, I believe you can make significant progress in this manner, but you can't reach the heights I know you want to reach if you rely solely on yourself. And you can't rely on yourself because the dreams in your heart are bigger than you. Furthermore, since we know our inside world creates our outside world, we also have to realize that our inside world can't always be trusted.

Why Your Mind Can't Be Trusted

Most people live by their minds, the little voice in their heads and the thoughts and feelings it produces. However, you can't always trust your mind. Now, it's not that your mind can't ever be trusted; it's that you trust it for the wrong things. You can trust it to help you see an oncoming car in traffic, to calculate a math problem or to write a report. But don't trust your mind to tell you what you need to hear. No – sometimes you need to do the talking.

Many self-help devotees, especially students of the Law of Attraction, keep trying to find a way to rely only on their minds and themselves. I've found it's better to count on things that are more reliable. And guess what's more reliable than ourselves?

You guessed it: The Creator of ourselves.

I've also concluded that when my confidence was only in myself, my goal was either too small, or my ego was too big. As contradictory as it may sound, I believe we all need to have a healthy feeling of weakness and dependence. Not to hinder us, but rather to strengthen us.

Control Isn't Conditional

Despite what some teachers declare, I will never believe I can control everything that happens to me. Why should I? The Bible explains: "in this world there will be trouble" and "many are the afflictions of the righteous". However, I do believe I can control how I *respond* and *interpret* everything that happens to me.

You need to decide upon a belief and philosophy and then live by it. If you believe you create everything that happens to you, then you must believe that all the time – no matter what happens. It's fine if you want to believe that way – just believe it consistently. The problem is that people are not consistent. They pick and choose from various teachings and philosophies to construct an incomplete foundation that doesn't hold up under attack.

How can you say **you** control the good things, but someone else controls the bad? It reminds me of parents who argue about their children, and one parent says, "Do you see what **your son** did in school today?" Or one parent says, "**Your daughter** got sent to the principal's office. What are **you** going to do about **her**?" If you believe you are 100% in control, then prepare to accept one-hundred percent responsibility for your life – positive *and* negative.

I believe I control a great portion of what happens in my life, but not all of it. I believe I sometimes reap where I didn't sow and sometimes I sow where I don't reap. I know there will be times on the road of life where I'm going to encounter an accident or traffic jam that will cause a delay. If I'm driving on the highway and there's an accident two miles ahead of me and traffic is backed up, am I going to blame myself? Did I manifest something that happened in the middle of the road that I'm traveling on?

Sometimes yes, many times not. The only thing I can do is keep my hand on the wheel and do everything in my power to continue in the direction I am heading. So listen, what I'm telling you is to <u>**stop beating yourself up**</u>. Stop re-evaluating your entire life over and over. Stop continually saying, "Oh, I must be using my thoughts or the Law of Attraction wrong because this showed up in my life and so I must have created it."

No, no, *no*! Stop looking in the rearview mirror all the time and just… keep… going!

There's a wonderful story to summarize the above points. Whatever you're doing right now, stop, slow down and take a deep breath. Grab something to drink and pretend you're sitting in front of a campfire on a pitch black night with a sky full of stars. The hustle and bustle of life is miles and miles away and you have an opportunity to listen to a wise teacher. Are you ready? As you imagine yourself by the campfire, focus and pay close attention so you'll never forget this lesson:

One evening, an old Cherokee told his grandson about a battle that goes on inside people everyday. He said, "My son, the battle is between two 'wolves' inside us all. One is Evil – It is anger, envy, jealousy, greed, and arrogance. The other is Good – It is peace, love, hope, humility, compassion and faith."

The grandson thought about this for a while and then asked his grandfather, "Which wolf wins?"

To which the old Cherokee simply replied, "The one you feed."

"Gonna Fly Now!"

Okay, the campfire is over. Put the marshmallows away because now it's back to training! I don't know about you, but I am a big Rocky fan. There is a part of the movie *Rocky III* that I feel illustrates this entire chapter better than anything else.

In *Rocky III*, we see what has become of the champion fighter. He was once an unknown, unranked and hungry fighter. Ironically, what initially put him in the spotlight was not a win, but rather a loss. The fact that he was able to go the distance and hang with then champion, Apollo Creed, set the stage for Rocky and everybody else that he may just be a bona fide fighter.

Then, in *Rocky II*, Apollo, who is certain it was a fluke Rocky was able to go the distance, arranges a rematch. Rocky prevails in the rematch and is catapulted to fame and fortune. Then (drum roll, please) we move into *Rocky III* territory and everything changes. Suddenly, Rocky feels secure in who he is and is winning fight after fight and defending his title over and over. That is, until Clubber Lang (Mr. T) enters the picture. (I pity the fool!)

Clubber challenges Rocky and ends up knocking him silly. However, the physical pain after the fight is nothing compared to the mental pain Rocky subsequently endures. The loss to Clubber Lang causes Rocky to doubt himself, his identity and everything he stands for.

He also learns that his manager, Mickey, had not always arranged the most challenging fights for Rocky. In fact, Mickey didn't even believe Rocky should have fought Clubber to begin with… which Rocky starts believing also. After some encouragement and coaxing from his new manager Apollo Creed (yes, the guy Rocky defeated became his manager), Rocky decides to go for a rematch against Clubber Lang.

As the training begins it is evident Rocky's head is somewhere else. He is only pushing himself on a moderate level and seems disinterested. The turning point of everything comes on a sandy beach on a beautiful day. Rocky and Apollo are supposed to be racing along the beach. As they begin sprinting, all Rocky can do is listen to the little voice in his head and visualize the "apparent" truth it is telling him.

Rocky fills his head with every negative, disempowering thought and image he can think of. He sees himself getting knocked down in the ring, he hears Mickey saying: "You can't win, Rock; he'll knock you 'til tomorrow. Hell, you ain't been hungry since you won that belt." This blast of negativity, fear and doubt seem to paralyze Rocky. So much so that he just gives up and stops running.

With a very disillusioned, dejected and depressed look on his face, Rocky stares out into the ocean. After a moment, his faithful wife Adrian walks up and asks if she can talk to him. She asks him questions (a lot of questions), trying to get to the root of what is going on. She finally begins to pierce the surface when Rocky says, "Nothing is real if you don't believe in who you are. I don't believe in myself no more, don't you understand?" He continues, "When a fighter don't believe in himself no more, that's it, it's over, that's it."

Adrian passionately responds with, "That's NOT it! Why don't you tell me the truth?"

Rocky says, "You want the truth? The truth is that I don't want to lose what I got."

After some explaining and justifying most of us would accept, Adrian still doesn't buy it. She says, "What do we have that can't be replaced? What, a house? We've got cars, we've got money, we've got everything but the truth. **What's the truth, dammit!?**"

At this point, Rocky surrenders to Adrian's award-winning interrogation techniques. Broken, he finally admits, "I'm afraid, all right? You want to hear me say it? You want to break me down? All right, I'm afraid. For the first time in my life, I'm afraid."

Adrian then offers some reasons why it doesn't matter if he's afraid and then says none of it's true anyway. She says, "It doesn't matter what I believe, because you're the one who's got to carry that fear around inside you. It doesn't matter if I tell you; it doesn't matter because you're the one who's gotta settle it. Get rid of it!"

She goes on, "Because when the smoke has cleared and everyone's through chanting your name, it's just gonna be us, and you can't live like this. *We* can't live like this. Because it's gonna bother you for the rest of your life. Look what it's doing to you now. I think you can do it, but you gotta do it for the right reasons. Not out of guilt, for the people, the money, or me. Just you, just you alone. If you lose, at least you lose with no excuses; no fear and I know you can live with that."

Let Me Be Your Adrian

The significance of this entire scene is: The only thing that changed about Rocky was what he **believed** about his circumstances and what he **believe**d about himself. It had everything to do with his identity, the identity that was stolen. The minute he was able to reconcile this inner belief and reclaim his identity, he was free. The minute he was able to admit his fear he could conquer it.

And the same thing can happen to you. You can say, "But yeah, that was only a movie." Well, I can tell you from experiences I have been through, seen and heard about all over the world that this scene better depicts real life for many people better than it ever serves as a scene in a movie.

The problem is most people don't have an Adrian who will persist until they get to the bottom of the root issue and, absent that, most people are simply too scared to pull back the layers themselves to get to the truth. Therefore, if it is okay with you, I am going to be your "Adrian" as we journey through this book together.

If we look closely at what put the fight back in Rocky, it had nothing to do with his physical ability; *it was all in his head.* What lie do you believe about yourself? What condition do you accept? What circumstance have you justified that's convinced you it's "okay" to accept things as they are? Or what do you want to give up on and say it's not meant to be? Do you mind if I ask you a question? **What's the truth, dammit?**

Tune In To Your Own "Whether Report"

If you watch the news each night, you'll see the weather report. Many people let this dictate what they will do, how they will feel, if they need the umbrella and if it will be a good day or a bad day. This is ridiculous on a lot of levels. However, people pay attention to another kind of "Whether Report" as well. And it can be far more damaging to your success than predicting the chances of a little rain or hot weather.

The "Whether Reports" most people tune into are not about precipitation or humidity, but the circumstances of life itself. They will believe in something, like or dislike something, go for something, or even dream something based on "whether this happens" or "whether that doesn't happen." A truly strong person will have personal goals backed with powerful beliefs and continue on the journey regardless of "whether" certain conditions happen or don't happen.

I think by now you see how critical the link is between your innermost thoughts and your physical actions. Whether it's Rocky feeling down on himself and performing poorly or you and me hearing our negative self-talk and not living our fullest lives, if we don't build a solid foundation where it counts most – inside – our outer lives will always be less than we want.

We've also looked at the issue of how much we control and how much we don't. This is important to consider as you journey through life, but know this: you are in control of your inner self.

In other words, what you believe really does determine what you can achieve. This inherent belief, rather than negative self-talk, the emotional baggage you picked up about yourself growing up and what someone else tells you to believe, should be the foundation upon which your self-image is built.

And since your belief is the key for which direction the oars of your conscious and subconscious mind take your life, we will cover it next.

Review

- Identity theft CAN be prevented.

- All upgrades in life begin with an upgrade in your self-image.

- Your mind can't always be trusted.

- We can't control everything, but we can control how we respond to everything.

- Which wolf wins? Fear and doubt can't survive if you starve them to death.

What's the truth, dammit!

3

WHERE THE WHEEL GOES, THE CAR FOLLOWS

*"Do not go where the path may lead;
go instead where there is no path and
leave a trail."*
~ Ralph Waldo Emerson

In this book we are going to cover a lot of "stuff." We'll cover your thoughts, words and actions. We'll discuss our feelings, our mentality and our spirit. All this "stuff" is great – grand, even – but it wasn't until I really had a "visual" for how my mind actually worked with all this "stuff" that I began to use it better – a *lot* better.

In this chapter, I want to talk to you about the interaction between your conscious and subconscious mind. If you were driving your car down the road and turned the steering wheel to the left, you would also expect your car to go to the left. Well, your mind works pretty much the same way. For new thoughts to really take root and begin the process of creating "things," they will have to be accepted by the subconscious mind.

The good news is that you don't have to be concerned or intimidated about figuring out your subconscious mind. You only have to be concerned with your conscious mind. Whatever the conscious mind accepts as true, your subconscious will also accept. Your subconscious will then go to work in ways beyond our comprehension to fulfill the belief. All we have to do is modify our conscious thinking so it is positive, empowering and in alignment with what we want. And implementing the perspectives you need to improve your conscious thoughts is what this chapter is about.

Think about your thoughts, feelings, emotions, words and beliefs as the "parts" inside your mind. Then think of your mind (your conscious and subconscious) as the "manufacturing plant" that assembles those "parts" into something useful.

All those parts are put together inside the plant – your mind. Somewhere in there, a very efficient processing plant (your mind) takes all these parts (your thoughts, feelings, emotions, doubts, fears, etc.) and "processes" them into a finished product, a result, goal or whatever it is you set out to do.

Lights, Camera, Action: How to Produce Your Own Life

Most of us know our minds work on two levels: the conscious and the subconscious. What most of us don't realize is how much sensitivity and power there are between the two. Your conscious mind is like a DVD and your subconscious mind is like a DVD player. A DVD player can't control what is put into it; and can only play what's on the DISC.

You can't put in a comedy and expect to see a thriller, or vice versa. What goes in is what comes out, period. Your DVD player will play the same movie over and over, unless, of course, you eject the old movie and play a new one. And who controls the content in the first place? Well, only the producer can control what goes into a movie. And in this case, guess who the producer is?

That's right: YOU! We will get more into the specifics of how to become an award-winning producer in just a bit. However, for now I want to make absolutely sure you understand how the "camera" works before you start taking pictures and recording any old thing.

Please make sure to let this idea of how your mind works sink in. Maybe think of it this way: just like construction workers can only build from the blueprint provided and an apple seed can only grow an apple, your subconscious mind can only create the thoughts and beliefs impressed upon it, right or wrong; good or bad. By clearly understanding this link between the conscious and subconscious mind, you will maximize your use of, and cooperation with, the Law of Attraction.

It Doesn't Have to Be True for You to Believe It

This chapter will change your life *if* you immerse yourself in its principles and not only learn them, but live them. Once you master these principles you will learn how to stop sabotaging your own progress and gain real influence and control over your mind. In fact, you *will* be able to transform every aspect of your life.

Is there really a "Secret"? Yes, I think there is, and it is simply learning how your conscious and subconscious work together. Once you master these skills, your life will take off like a rocket. The good news is that you already have this power. And even better, the formula you need to grab hold of your mind and influence your thinking is actually quite simple.

In basic math we learn 2 +2 = 4. That seems elementary to most, but for a person who has never had basic math, 2 + 2 might actually prove quite difficult. Learning how to use your mind and especially how to capitalize on belief really *is* a simple formula.

I have already expressed my belief in God, so take this next statement at face value for purposes of this example. I learned this from Joseph Murphy: "It is not the thing believed in, but the belief within your own mind that brings about the result." Placebo tests are a good way to illustrate the principle described.

Here is a simple snapshot of how your mind works: Anything you believe with your conscious mind is what your subconscious mind will accept. When your subconscious mind accepts the belief or thought, it begins to execute a plan to bring the thought into reality. All your thoughts and beliefs are recorded onto your conscious mind (DVD) and then your subconscious mind (DVD player) plays it out as your reality and it shows up on your TV screen.

My subconscious mind has produced some serendipitous outcomes, victories, opportunities, relationships and some amazing "coincidences". But I believe my subconscious usually delivers what I program in two primary ways:

1. By providing ideas

2. By allowing me to see what already exists

I think many people go wrong when they try to apply mental laws and manipulate their thinking without realizing what *they* are responsible for. For example, Michael Jordan certainly visualized the ball going in the net, but he still had to shoot the ball.

When it comes to ideas, I think most people underestimate their value. Ideas are everything. All advances in life have been the result of new ideas being acted upon. It was an idea that moved us from horse and buggy to the current amazing advancement of the automobile.

We've moved from telegraphs to iPhones, black and white TV to Satellite TV. This trend of never-ending external advancement will continue in the future because of the men and women who are committed to never ending internal (mental/spiritual) advancement.

So when you begin to think about what you want for the purposes of programming your conscious mind (which in turn programs your subconscious mind), you need to keep your eyes wide open for ideas that are delivered to you. They are the primary means by which you will turn your thoughts into things, and it is pretty obvious by simply looking around that new ideas are being delivered… and acted upon all the time.

Here are just a few examples of ideas, both past and present:

- Facebook
- YouTube
- Twitter
- The Space shuttle
- iPod
- Tivo
- The Internet
- A microwave
- Golf (and any other sport)
- Reality shows

Almost everything started as an idea. That's why the leaders of yesterday, today and tomorrow don't get rattled by external circumstances such as the economy, global warming or anything most of us "mere mortals" worry about. Why? They know ideas are king... and kings rule!

You don't need to know much about your subconscious mind to get better use of it. In fact, many people generate wonderful results from their subconscious minds every day – and don't even realize it. And, of course, the opposite is also true. When we *don't* tap into our subconscious at the levels available to us, we're only working at half-capacity – probably even less than that. So, we aren't going to take that chance and remain in the dark any longer.

Let's keep going and figure this out.

You will certainly notice that most of the chapters in this book are closely related. Your beliefs, identity and the workings of your conscious and subconscious mind are closely connected and have many interchangeable concepts. In the "Jailbreak" section of Chapter 6, I will talk about judges and juries. Well, let's back up a little. Specifically, let's talk about the jury selection process. If you have ever been in a jury pool, you've noticed the attorneys for both sides ask potential jurors about their beliefs. But why would *beliefs* matter if the lawyers are able to present the *facts* to the jury?

Attorneys for both sides know that regardless of the evidence (facts) presented during the trial, a person's subconscious beliefs will pre-determine if the juror even "sees" the evidence, much less believes it. Attorneys know the juror's subconscious mind will skip over it, remain blind to it and even ignore it if the person already has a particular belief about something. The lawyers know that anything potential jurors currently believe is what they will likely continue to believe before, during and long after the trial is over – no matter how much convincing evidence they present.

Your subconscious mind will also make sure your thoughts, actions, mannerisms and behaviors match your beliefs. This is one of the main reasons your outside world is reflected by your inside.

The vast majority of people who thought OJ Simpson was innocent (or guilty) *before* his "trial of the century" had the same beliefs *after* the trial. And it was a trial with more than one year of evidence, witnesses and testimony.

The Strangest Secret

I wish I was giving you a breakthrough idea in this chapter. Instead I hope to finally, once and for all, convince you of what you already know to be true, but just keep wondering if there might be something you're missing. There isn't. Your inside world *does* create your outside world. I wish I had some new technology to introduce. I wish I had found some hidden key to success and happiness. Unfortunately – and fortunately – we can search the world over for the answer that will change our lives and we will always come back to the inescapable fact that our inside world will continue to create our outside world. This is good news. So stop searching and start mastering.

In the landmark personal development recording "The Strangest Secret," the late Earl Nightingale reconciles this same issue. He provides the following eerily ironic documentation that person after person has concluded the same thing as he had. Here is an excerpt of his commentary:

> *Marcus Aurelius, the great Roman Emperor, said: "A man's life is what his thoughts make of it."*
>
> *Disraeli said this: "Everything comes if a man will only wait … a human being with a settled purpose must accomplish it, and nothing can resist a will that will stake even existence for its fulfillment."*
>
> *William James said: "We need only in cold blood act as if the thing in question were real, and it will become infallibly real by growing into such a connection with our life that it will become real. It will become so knit with habit and emotion that our interests in it will be those which characterize belief." He continues, " … only you must, then, really wish these things, and wish them exclusively, and not wish at the same time a hundred other incompatible things just as strongly."*

My old friend Dr. Norman Vincent Peale put it this way: "If you think in negative terms, you will get negative results. If you think in positive terms, you will achieve positive results."

George Bernard Shaw said: "People are always blaming their circumstances for what they are. I don't believe in circumstances. The people who get on in this world are the people who get up and look for the circumstances they want, and if they can't find them, make them."

Well, it's pretty apparent, isn't it? We become what we think about. A person who is thinking about a concrete and worthwhile goal is going to reach it, because that's what he's thinking about. Conversely, the person who has no goal, who doesn't know where he's going, and whose thoughts must therefore be thoughts of confusion, anxiety, fear, and worry will thereby create a life of frustration, fear, anxiety and worry.

And if he thinks about nothing ... he becomes nothing.

I Still Haven't Found What I'm looking for

I've spent much of my time on this planet looking for something else – looking for some magic bullet, some critical key that would unlock everything for me. If only I'd spent that time studying how to work with my inside world instead of looking for something in the outside world, I would have achieved things much faster – and easier. My search taught me one thing: the inside is the key and the key is in the inside.

So remember, your subconscious construction crew can only build what is on the blueprint. From time to time, your construction crew will get ahead of schedule or behind schedule. This is usually a result of your inconsistent thoughts – which lead to inconsistent actions. However, your subconscious will always try to correct for mistakes. It will always work to reconcile circumstances so they get back to the blueprint. It will always work toward your comfort zone and to the idea of what is normal and right *for you.*

This is the ultimate conflict in our brain and a concept that must be dealt with and broken through. It's why people with the best intentions struggle to make changes. It's why your subconscious will get you back into debt if that's what you programmed it to do.

If you program your subconscious that you want to get out of debt, and then you become debt-free, you need to program it to invest or do something different, etc. Otherwise, if left to its' own devices, your subconscious will do what it's always done and get you back into debt!

It's the same with weight loss and anything else you can think of. Unless you change what *was* normal for you, then your mind will always take you back there. The best way to begin changing the "old" normal and give your conscious mind a new blueprint for your subconscious mind to work on is to set new goals and clarify your purpose. We'll discuss this in upcoming chapters.

Have you ever wanted to get a new job so you could get a fresh start? Or maybe you've wanted to move to a new neighborhood, church or even another state so you could start over? If you followed through with any of these steps, then you probably discovered there's a lot of truth to the saying, "Wherever you go, there you are." What this means is you really can't escape and start over because wherever you go, you take yourself with you!

However, there are circumstances where "flip-flopping" the whole inside-outside theory can work for you. Now, wait a minute! Haven't I been saying, unequivocally, the inside affects the outside? Yes, I have, and yes, it does. But, sometimes, there are exceptions. Sometimes your inside can benefit by a little (or a big) boost from the outside.

Change the Outside First!

Let's consider what happens when you change all or part of your outside world first, such as a relationship, your environment, etc. Think about the times you have purchased a new car, a new watch or some new clothes. Can you remember how it made you feel? I remember several times when I got a new car or new clothes. They were external changes and made me feel better on the outside which, in turn, affected how I felt on the inside.

One of the most profound examples I see is with the TV show, Extreme Makeover: Home Edition. In this show people fall to pieces and erupt with tears of joy over their external change. The new home they acquire gives them hope, excitement and a new attitude. But I believe there is a catch. The recipients of these homes have one of two choices to make. They can begin to raise their self-image and see themselves as someone who lives in their new home, or they can keep their current self-image and see themselves as the person who lived in the other home. This decision is critical, and here is why. Some people will raise the quality of their inside world to correspond with the new home and standard of living on the outside. Others will lower the quality of their outside world to correspond with their old standard of living on the inside. Some people receive the wonderful gift of a new home and it creates internal changes along with it. Others can't handle it. They don't take care of the home; they get into debt and fall right back where they feel they belong and where they see themselves on the inside.

The Seed and the Soil: Growth is a Process

What I want to introduce at this point are some areas where I think people make mistakes in applying this "inner-world-creating-outer-world" principle and how it influences the conscious and subconscious mind. Many people agree with this concept without hesitation. And that is part of the problem. What do I mean? Here's an example: Sure, what you plant in your mind is what you get. **But not instantly**. There is, in fact, a growth process. Many people make this mistake. They don't realize (or have completely forgotten) they have planted the seed.

They think about what they want and go on with life, expecting it to manifest right away. Then, when it doesn't materialize within a suitable time frame, they abort the mission and begin to doubt themselves and the power of their minds.

As a result, those buds of intention, desire or wanting wither and die on the vine. It's no different than planting a seed, watering it for a few days and abandoning it when it fails to spring up into an orange tree practically overnight. Is it any surprise when you come back a week or two later to find the soil is dry, the leaves are brown and the seed is quite dead?

You must have faith that, with continued water and care, the seed *will* grow, even if you can't actually see that growth with your very own eyes. My own personal power slowly evolved through many stages of faith and doubt and, finally, landed in a place that worked for me.

This strong mentality came from my belief that my seed was *in* the ground – *not* because I could see my goal. If we already have something or can already see something, then we don't need to believe it anyway. I like to stand back and look at my life from the outside. If what I want hasn't borne fruit yet,

I just say, "Oh well, the seed is in the ground. I am thinking about it, so it is still growing."

"If you want to make an apple pie from scratch,
you must first create the universe."
~ Carl Sagan

The problem is we tend to make very unrealistic rules for how long something should take and, frankly, who are we to make those rules? This next fact gave me an incredible amount of patience because of how much I always related to the seed and soil analogy. If you plant an apple seed, you get apples, right? But do you know how long it actually takes for an apple tree to go from seed to fruit? And I am talking about the normal course of nature; the way God set it up, not a nursery grafting a tree! It can take anywhere from six to ten years! Man, did *that* change my perspective.

Many of us give up on a goal prematurely, saying to ourselves, "I planted that goal and it has been two days, two weeks or even two years and I don't have it yet. This stuff doesn't work!" Look, if we are going to apply the seed and soil philosophy to our lives, then we have to apply the **whole** philosophy, not just the parts we like or the parts that work quickly for us. You can't acknowledge that there is "seed time" and "harvest time" and ignore that there is "growth time."

Yes, a seed goes into the ground and it bears fruit. But in between is a long, incredibly boring and not-much-to-watch growth process. It's the same with your goals. You plant what you want and wait to see it bear fruit, but you need to *believe* through each phase of the growth process, and not expect to skip from seed to harvest.

Not only do we need to have a good perspective about how the growing of our goal parallels the growth of a seed, we also need to have a good perspective about how our goal parallels the actual planting of the seed in the first place. What happens when we plant something? The seed is shoved into the ground and buried in the cold, dark mud. There is not much oxygen down there and it's hard to get the air it needs to grow.

You might wonder how it survives down there. Well, guess what? It doesn't! This insight gave me a new perspective. A seed (goal) doesn't get buried and fight its way out. Instead, the seed gives its life so something new can grow. It's a lot like shedding our past beliefs to make room for something new. It may be hard and some beliefs don't always mesh with others, but in order for a new belief to live, an old belief must surely give way.

How you handle and respond to circumstances, adversity and even success during the growth process is one of the key factors in your success. Anybody can plant. And anybody can give up on the seed they planted, leaving it to dry out and wither from lack of proper care and feeding. The challenge, I believe, lies more in our interpretation (and often our *misinterpretation*) of what is *really* taking place in the growth process. If we receive rain (metaphorically speaking) and try to escape it (when it is exactly what we need to grow), then we may escape the success we ultimately seek.

> *"Anyone can count the seeds in an apple, but only*
> *God can count the number of apples in a seed."*
> **~ Robert H. Schuller**

Again, it comes down to what you believe as opposed to what you can see. Would you say your life is on track, or off track? Well, hold up: what exactly is "on" or "off," and who decides? Do you suppose it's possible for you to *think* you are off track and, by thinking you are off track, you actually *get* off track? You bet it is! Far too many times people are exactly where they need to be, but because they don't see their expected results they stop watering, fertilizing and pulling the weeds out of the garden of their goals and dreams.

I bet many of you are reading this book because you think you are off track, when actually you aren't. Some of you may be trying to fix something that isn't broken. Some of you are trying to dig something up that needs to stay in the ground. Some of you need to stop beating yourself up, and become a little more upbeat.

Could You Already Be in the Perfect Spot?

Have you spent a lot of time and money on personal development? Have you taken business risks – and lost? Have you read books on how to build wealth or build a business – yet you're still struggling financially or maybe even in debt? Would you be willing to accept a different perspective for a few moments? It's okay; if you don't like it, you don't have to keep it. You can keep it if you want, or you can just throw it out.

What if you were to stop right now and declare that you are in the perfect spot? That you are exactly where you should be? Isn't it true that most of the frustration you experience is tied to unmet expectations? What are expectations? Are they facts? Or are they beliefs about the "who, what, when and where" someone or something should be?

> *"I know I'm getting better at golf because*
> *I'm hitting fewer spectators."*
> **~Gerald Ford**

I have a friend named Matt who once worked for one of my businesses. He happened to be a pretty good golfer too. Matt was an account executive and lost his temper very quickly when things didn't go his way or get done in the time frame he expected. Now, I had much more experience than Matt and I had a different perspective. I thought he was doing a great job and things were going appropriately. Well, one day he threw some files at me (he won't admit it, though) because he'd lost his temper again.

I looked him in the eye and said, "Matt, if you're on the golf course and you're playing a par four and you make it in three shots, how do you feel?" (Note to non-golfers: The main object of golf is to get the little white ball in the hole. A hole is also classified by its par, which is the number of strokes a skilled golfer should require to complete the play of a hole. You are happy when you hit par or under and not happy when you don't!) Let's get back to the story…

He said, "Great."

Then I said, "If you are playing on a par five and make it in ten shots, how do you feel?"

He said, "Not as good. I may throw my clubs."

I responded and told him what his problem was. I said, "This job is a par 4 course and you are making the shots in three strokes. But you're acting and believing like you're playing a par five and taking ten shots."

How many times do we set up the golf course of our own lives and miscalculate the par (and I am not talking about being average here) and live in constant frustration as a result of our own misguided perceptions?

After Matt changed his belief about what par was for him, he became more productive than before and was more relaxed and happy. Funny how that works. He also stopped chain smoking and throwing stuff at me too. All this happened without changing the clubs, changing the ball, the cart or anything else. It was just a change of perspective.

If you could, would you take back all the money you've invested in your business and exchange it for everything you have learned? What about your investment in books, seminars, audio programs or any other professional development? Would you take back the money you've invested to gain education by traveling to seminars, staying in hotels, renting cars and eating in restaurants? I didn't think so. You need to see yourself just as you would see any business, and especially a start-up business. Start-up businesses aren't suppose to make a profit right away, and even the most established tree in the forest is barren for a short time each year.

I don't care if it has been one year, three years, five years or more since you started working on this "business" of YOU and developing yourself. The longer you spend and the deeper a foundation you build, the greater your profit anyway. I love what Brian Tracy says, "The height to which you rise will be determined by the depth to which you develop yourself."

Your bank account may be low but you are not broke; your money is simply invested and tied up in various aspects of the venture you are funding and are continuing to build and grow. The best news is that all your time, energy and investing is guaranteed to bring intangible returns and the intangible returns (inside) create the tangible returns (outside) anyway.

I implemented my own version of this idea when I went to seminars. I used to go to seminars to find that *one idea* that could change everything. I don't do that anymore. My objective is not to find what's wrong. My goal is only to refine, improve, and grow — one seminar, one speaker, one book, one audiotape and one idea at a time. There's nothing missing. There's nothing wrong.

We want things too quickly and, in the very wanting itself, we destroy those things we yearn for. It's okay to want, but it's also important to realize that what we want needs time to grow. So do we.

Let's Go Into the Recording Studio:

That's where Production Begins!

Let's wrap up Chapter 3 with those tips on becoming an award-winning producer. These ideas will be somewhat related to the Success Compass System in Part 2. In the meantime, this section will serve as an excellent foundation and give you a better understanding of how to influence the conscious and subconscious mind.

We will begin by taking a closer look at our DVD metaphor. It provides an excellent but simple example of how your mind works. In fact, you can begin to make immediate improvements in any area of life by implementing these steps. For the purpose of our example we will break things down in the following manner:

Think of your **conscious mind** as a DVD disc.

Think of your **subconscious mind** as a DVD player.

Think of your **reality** as what shows up on the TV screen.

It may help to see the following visual for each of the above:

DVD	**DVD Player**	**TV Screen**
Conscious Mind	*Sub-Conscious Mind*	*Reality*

Remember, whatever shows up on the TV screen of life (your reality) is what was recorded on the DVD. In other words, you can't put in a *Transformers* DVD and expect to see *Pretty Woman*. What was recorded, printed and shipped on the DVD is what will show up on the TV screen, regardless of what you want to see. So that is where we will start. In contrast to producing a movie, the only recording device we need is a pen and paper.

Let's say you wanted a higher income to show up on *your* screen of life. You now know you would begin by upgrading your "inside" world. You would upgrade your self-image, self-esteem, etc. and then ultimately set goals to correspond with what you wanted to accomplish. You would also begin to write down your goals (i.e. begin recording on your DVD).

For example, you may write something along the lines of:

My life is improving every day. I am advancing, progressing and getting wealthier every day. I earn XYZ per year and it comes to me at various times in various amounts as I give excellent service to my clients.

You might then collect some pictures of things you would buy with your increased income. Your subconscious doesn't know the difference between something that actually happened versus something that was vividly imagined. If you keep pictures around of things you want, your subconscious will start to feel that you have it and will figure out a way for you to have it.

By writing your goals, affirming, and visualizing them you are "burning" them onto the DVD (your conscious mind), and also putting them into the DVD player (subconscious mind). By doing this over and over, by making it a habitual behavior, the recordings on your DVD will show up on the screen of life as your **reality**.

A real DVD player has to spin the DVD consistently for it to play. Our life is the same way. Our version of spinning is thinking about our goals, writing them down, affirming, visualizing and, of course, taking action. Once we do that, there is nothing else the TV can broadcast. Remember, your DVD player (subconscious mind) has to play what has been recorded. It then shows up as your reality (your TV screen of life).

Troubleshooting Guide

Every DVD player – or other piece of high-tech electronic equipment – comes with a troubleshooting guide to help you with any problems. Real life is no different; here are some ways to troubleshoot various problems that pop up from time to time:

- **Problem**: There is nothing on my screen. (i.e. I don't yet have my desires or goals.)

- **Answer**: Is the power on? Have you pushed Pause, Stop or, even worse, Rewind? If there is still nothing on your screen, please review the recording process carefully and try again. It probably means you haven't recorded anything besides the opening credits and now you have a blank screen.

- **Recommendations**: Finish this book!

- **Problem**: The picture freezes or skips.

- **Solution**: There may be a scratch on your DVD. Are you believing one day and doubting the next?

- **Recommendations**: Finish this book!

- **Problem**: What I recorded on my DVD is not what is showing on my screen.

- **Solution**: Keep watching; some movies are longer than others. If your movie is still playing, then it must be good! It takes awhile for a good plot to unfold.

- **Recommendations**: Finish this book!

Well, that's all for your crash course in movie production. Practice these tips and apply them to what you learn in Part 2 and you will be creating a Blockbuster movie in no time!

Review

- Whatever your conscious mind accepts as true, your subconscious mind will also accept. Your subconscious will go to work to fulfill the belief.

- A seed of "thought" must grow the corresponding "thing," just as an apple seed must grow an apple.

- Ideas are king and kings rule.

- Everything you want already exists. You don't need to create it. You simply need to align your thinking with what you want and then what you want will begin to show up.

- There is seed time, harvest time and, of course, growth time.

What is your PAR?

4

LET'S POP THE HOOD!

"Life is like a 10 speed bicycle,
most of us have gears we never use."
~ Charlie Brown

In Chapter 3, we learned how to better steer the direction of our lives by getting the most out of our conscious and subconscious minds. In Chapter 4, we are going to pop the hood of your head and do a diagnostic analysis of what is going on in there!

God has never spoken to me.

What I mean is I have never audibly heard His voice. In fact, I used to look at people kind of weird when they said, "God told me this" or "God told me that." I think I still do.

My point is this: even though I haven't audibly "heard" God's voice, I believe He communicates with me and reveals His presence through my journaling, word pictures and analogies that make things clearer. In fact, much of my mental and spiritual growth has come in these ways.

For example, it was my daughter's second birthday and she got all kinds of cool toys. One toy in particular, which appeared to be the coolest of all, needed a certain kind of battery we didn't have on hand. To prevent the world from coming to an end, I did what any good father would do: I jumped in my car and headed for the nearest convenience store!

As I drove, I realized the cool and exciting toy was absolutely futile without batteries. Without a power source, it was basically no more than an abstract and senseless piece of plastic. However, once we put the batteries in, it came to life with noises, lights and colors. It was the same toy as before and you couldn't even *see* what made it different. The batteries were tucked away underneath, out of sight but absolutely significant to making things work.

Hopefully, you can see the parallel I am drawing. This lesson hit me like a ton of bricks. It gave me a new way to view the spiritual side of life. Despite the extravagant and surreal design of the human body, it too becomes a futile device without its power source. This seemingly simple lesson brought the awareness of my spirit much closer to my consciousness. I thought, "This spirit (or spiritual) side of me is not *somewhere out there*; turns out it is something *right in here*."

Batteries Included!

Then I began to realize that, far from being something separate or oblique, my spirit is so prominent in my life that if "the batteries" were removed, everything would stop — immediately. My heart wouldn't beat, my eyes wouldn't see, my ears wouldn't hear and on and on. I would be no more than an empty shell. Just stopping to think about this gave me a different perspective and appreciation of my spiritual life.

And that is what I want to give you.

The Law of Attraction begins when you understand that what you are and who you are is deeply embedded not in your *body*, not in your *mind*, but deep in your *spirit*. It wasn't until I made the leap from seeing myself as a physical body to seeing myself as a living, energized spirit that I was able to make significant progress in all areas of my life, including the Law of Attraction.

This concept can be covered in unbelievable detail, from the most basic principles all the way up to the complex. This includes, but is not limited to, quantum physics, quarks and subatomic particles. But I don't like to overcomplicate things.

When I stop and think about what makes my heart beat, controls my breathing, makes my hair and fingernails grow, allows my eyes to see and my ears to hear, I'm blown away. I also find it pretty coincidental that we need oxygen to breathe, water to drink and food to eat — and it's all just naturally and "coincidentally" available on this little planet we call earth. Another awe-inspiring concept is when I get a cut or broken bone, my body is automatically equipped to heal it. Furthermore, I think God topped it all off by proving man's divine nature in our ability to think.

All other forms of life rely on instinct. If we are to believe in evolution, then why hasn't my cat learned to drive and why hasn't a third, fourth or fifth sex come into the picture? Why aren't dogs coming up with ideas for cell phones or surfing the Internet?

In addition to pondering these questions, I needed to reconcile the whole idea of someone being raised from the dead. I came to this conclusion: If I, myself, was born, then at one time I was not alive. If I was not alive, I was dead. Therefore, when I was born I was essentially raised from the dead. If God can bring us to life in the first place, why is it so difficult to believe that He could raise someone from the dead?

These ideas are about as complex as I'd like to get. The reason it's important to see yourself as a spirit rather than just a body is because doing so will give you faith, confidence and ultimate power. When most of us take inventory of ourselves, we find all kinds of weaknesses, faults and limitations. However, our spirit side is unlimited. ***The God of the Universe***, who created everything, tells us He made us in ***His*** image. Being created in His image includes many profound things. I have personally found the idea of having access to an ***invisible source of unlimited and creative power*** to be incredibly significant.

When you become consciously aware of your spirit and see yourself and approach life with this perspective, it allows your thoughts to rise higher and your beliefs to soar. And this is where real change begins. Your current level of thinking, talking and believing has brought you to where you are right now – today. Only by improving those areas on the inside can you improve things on the outside. Improvement starts when you begin to see yourself differently than you have in the past.

Energize Your Spirit

When Einstein discovered the concept of mass-energy equivalence or $E = mc2$ (energy equals mass multiplied by the speed of light squared) he introduced the idea that the world is made up of only two things: energy and matter. He further proved that neither matter nor energy can be created or destroyed. Both matter and energy can be transformed, but neither can be destroyed.

In the book *Think and Grow Rich*, Napoleon Hill concluded: "If life is anything at all, it has got to be energy. If neither energy nor matter can be destroyed, of course life cannot be destroyed. Life, like other forms of energy, may be passed through various processes of transition, or change, but it cannot be destroyed. Therefore, even death is only a transition." These principles become even more significant when combined with the realization of how thoughts become things; ***thoughts are energy and things are matter***.

This entire formula gave me the understanding I needed to appreciate how we could actually create with our thoughts. It gave me reason to not only believe in the great truth that we become what we think about, but to know ***how*** and ***why***.

Einstein demonstrated and proved that energy and mass are equivalent; they are essentially two sides of the same coin. His formula showed mass can be converted into energy and energy can be converted into mass. The formula has been used most notably to show how much energy would be released if a certain amount of mass was converted into energy, thus the idea for the atomic bomb.

Even the tiniest piece of mass has the potential to give off a vast amount of energy. It's the kind of energy we can't even imagine – the kind of energy scientists and physicists spend their entire careers studying.

I think of Einstein's theory every time I picture the tiniest goal, desire or dream buried in the human heart. If we only knew (and now we do) that our very spirits have the capacity to connect with God's infinite intelligence and set forces in motion that are beyond anything we could ever do on our own. He equipped us with divine power to create what we desire by using our minds. He provided us with the amazing ability to direct our thoughts, which ultimately organizes energy, which in turn converts into conditions, events and circumstances.

The problem is that few of us believe this about ourselves. We don't believe that our spirits and thoughts are as powerful as they are. We forget that they are a part of us. We get stuck in our everyday circumstances and doubt that we can begin a new life by adopting new thoughts.

The most reassuring aspect of Einstein's theory is that energy is the true commerce of the universe. All things come from, transmit and *are* energy: a light beam, a desk lamp, a steam engine, an atom bomb, a field mouse or a human being. It's reassuring because we know the world of spirit and the world of form are not separate. They are two different aspects of one existence and we only need to cooperate with them.

In his last interview with Barbara Walters nine months before he died, Patrick Swayze answered candid questions about life and death. He talked about what supported his belief in the spirit and soul. He reminded viewers it is a recorded fact that our flesh and bones cannot contain the electrical energy that physically operates our bodies. He said this fact serves as evidence of a physical, tangible and real sign of a soul. I also like what Napoleon Hill said. He proclaimed proof of a spirit by the fact that we receive ideas from somewhere other than the five senses.

Each and every one of us is a force to be reckoned with, no matter how small we sometimes may feel. You should not see yourself as an infinitesimal speck on the backside of the planet; rather you should see yourself as a spirit full of energy. As you concentrate on your life's direction, you transmit and organize energy to bring it into being. This is you directly influencing the universe. Believe it!

The Mystery of Life

The Bible tells us not to lean on our own understanding. So guess what? I'm not going to! Part of life is going to be a mystery. Even if you are a committed Christian believer and trust every word of the Bible, there are still mysteries. I can buy the story that God made me, but who made God? How exactly did God get the power to create? If I let it, questioning could boggle my mind. No wonder He told us to lean on Him and not ourselves.

I believe you have to leave room for unknowns in any philosophy. For example, we don't know exactly how our minds work, but we know they work. Sure, scientists might give you an answer. But if you keep peeling back layers you get to a place that says, "Yes, I understand all that, but how does *that* work?" At the end of the day you have to ask yourself this question: Did you create yourself? NO! If not, then someone else did. Trust "Them."

Moving forward, we need to agree "how this all works" remains a mystery. What's important is that it does work. We matter; our matter matters. I don't want you spending the rest of this book scratching your head, ignoring all these life-changing principles because you're still overly concerned with *how* this works.

I want you to concentrate on what you're learning so that by the time you've finished this book, you'll agree that it does work, whether you understand the "how" or not. And of course, I believe it works better when we include God and any missing links as opposed to leaving them out.

A note before we continue: You've probably noticed I reference some concepts that are religious or spiritual and some that are scientific. This doesn't mean I am confused about my beliefs. Everyone's spiritual growth evolves through different means and timeframes. In my personal journey of spiritual growth, I discovered many scientific ideas that have given me more faith in God, not less.

Let me quote Einstein again and I think you'll see where I am coming from: "Science without religion is lame. Religion without science is blind."

Three Parts to Make a Whole: Physical, Mental and Spiritual

If you learn nothing else from this chapter, I hope you learn we are not just physical beings. We are also mental and spiritual.

Even though most people acknowledge this fact, they don't give all three parts equal attention.

People eat breakfast, lunch and dinner. They shower, primp and spend an hour getting ready for work every day. They go to the soccer game, the mall and spend hours in front of the TV. However, most people devote very little time to their spiritual sides (which is the root of creation) and wonder why they have external struggles. We have to stop feeding only the physical side and give appropriate heed to the mental and spiritual sides.

We are all the sum of three parts:

1. **Physical**: Our bodies merely serve as the vehicles that move our spirits down the road of life. The Bible tells us our bodies are temples that hold our spirit. If we compare it to the earlier example of my daughter's new toy, our physical being is like the plastic, wiring, lights and shiny paint of her brand-new toy. As a transition point, I like what George Melton said, "The body is an instrument, the mind its function, the witness and reward of its operation."

2. **Mental**: Our mental state is the diplomat between the physical and the spiritual. Our brain moves our legs through electrical – there goes that energy again – impulses. Thoughts, too, are mere energy that form lucid theories in our brains. How we think, act, speak and socialize is our spirit at work in the world. To revisit the

toy analogy, our mental state is the knowledge, wisdom and inspiration needed to create the toy, package the batteries and put them on the market. However, a very important distinction to make is that *you* are not *your mind*. Your mind is a tool of your body, much like your hand or your legs. The mind's function is to think, reason, etc. It is not you. Making this distinction alone has unlocked greater potential for many people.

3. **Spiritual**: Finally, we usually ignore the most important aspect of who we are. Our spirit is the "be-all and end-all" of who – and what – we are. As I mentioned earlier, it is our spirit, the power in the batteries so to speak, that keeps us alive. It is the grand mystery of what created us and it is the inspiration for every thought we have. Try taking your "batteries" (your spirit) out – you'd be a blank slate. You'd be standing in the corner with no life, light or legitimate reason for being. Our spirits fill us with everything and anything we need. I love what the French philosopher, Pierre Teilhard said: "We are not human beings having a spiritual experience; we are spiritual beings having a human experience."

Acknowledge – and Energize – Your Spirit

Obviously, we can't control or completely understand God, His mystery or His infinite wisdom. However, we can control our spirits or, more specifically, we can acknowledge that our spirits not only exist but are our very reason for being. We can recognize that our spirits provide the energy for us to live and, as we have learned, energy is life.

In closing Chapter 4, here are some thoughts that help me keep all this stuff in perspective: God created the world. He created the world by thinking and speaking it into existence. For example, God said, "Let there be light." Look outside tomorrow morning and let me know what you see! I guess it worked.

There also must be energy behind what God did. Do you think there is some energy behind the sun and the earth spinning on its axis? Now, the Bible says we are made in God's image. So, in the interest of keeping it as simple, it clearly seems to make sense that if we are made in His image, and all things are made of energy, then we should be able to create our own world in a similar fashion and sequence: through thinking and speaking it and by using our energy – our thought energy.

Let's move on to Chapter 5 and learn how.

Review

- Our spirit is not somewhere "out there."

- We are created in God's image, which includes a limitless and abundant nature.

- Everything in the world is made up of only two things: energy and matter.

- Thoughts are energy and things are matter.

- Do not lean on your own understanding.

5

THESE ARE THE ROADS, HERE ARE THE DIRECTIONS

"You can have anything you want if you will give up the belief that you can't have it."
~ **Dr. Robert Anthony**

Many people think the Law of Attraction is a recent fad made famous by a wildly popular video and a slew of resulting bestsellers. In reality, the wisdom needed to attain a life of joy, success, happiness and abundance in every area of life has been around forever.

Why then, do people still struggle with becoming joyful, successful, happy and abundant? Why are there so many unhappy, negative, confused, frustrated and hurting people in the world today when the knowledge to be anything but is right at their fingertips?

Furthermore, why do some people work hard their whole lives and still struggle financially, while others, with less talent and less effort, create abundance in the area of finances and live rich, fruitful lives? Of course, we witness this in all areas of life, not just financial.

In the past, these issues confused and concerned me, especially when I saw the impact they had on the good, hardworking Christians in my life. I mean, how can bad things, including financial struggles, happen to a super nice, intelligent, church-going person? Where is the justice in *that*?

This no longer confuses or concerns me because I finally learned that God's word, and all words for that matter, are neutral. Now, before you wonder if I got struck by lightning for using a word like "neutral" to describe the words of our Creator, let me give you a quick example.

Think of it this way: it's kind of like the notes on a sheet of music. They are neutral; they are just sitting there. They may come from hours of inspired composing, but for now they are just specks of black ink on a white page. To come to life again, to produce the beautiful music shown on the sheet, those musical notes need a catalyst. Once the instrument used by a human begins to play them, those musical notes actually do what they were written to do. Then, of course, each musician performs at a different level.

While some notes of music barely stir in the hands of a casual novice or sag while played by an inexperienced or uninterested student, other musical notes can make beautiful – almost divine impressions when played in the hands of a master or, for that matter, the inspired.

The best way to support what I am saying is with the revered words in Proverbs 23:7: "As a man thinks in his heart, so is he." From the *good book*, the first book, and the real all-time bestseller comes the *true* Law of Attraction. Whether a man thinks great, good, average, poor, evil, etc., ***that is what will be***.

This Proverb provides more evidence to show us we do play a significant role in creating our lives. Now, I don't mean to contradict anything I've said up to this point, but you could certainly ponder a reversal on a very popular book that may sort of explain "Why **good** things happen to **bad** people." This may also explain the words: "He makes His sun rise on the evil and the good and sends rain on the just and the unjust."

I had the privilege of sharing lunch with Zig Ziglar several years ago at a seminar. He said something I will never forget: There were about 8 of us gathered at a table with him and somebody fired a question that elicited this response "We don't always get what we deserve…"

Of course, I expected the direction of his comment to provide some motivation and perspective on how to face adversity and obstacles. Instead he finished with "… and I'm grateful for that." Then he delivered a much-needed reminder of how often we are the undeserving recipients of God's immeasurable grace. We will never figure out all of God's ways so we just have to work with them the best we can and if we do our best to heed his Word, then we can be the catalyst for our own change.

Got a Problem? Don't Look for Help – Look Under the Hood!

If you're reading this book, it's probably safe to assume there is a goal you want to accomplish, a challenge you want to overcome, or a relationship you want to improve, eliminate or create. It's also probably safe to say you have things in your life you never wanted, and you want things you've never had.

The most common misunderstanding in the entire world is trying to solve our problems from the wrong end. If you look at the mortgage and auto industry crisis today, you will notice the proposed strategies for solving the problems are all related to external solutions.

Both industries wrongly assume that by dumping more money in from the outside the problem will magically be solved. But when leaders of the big three auto companies fly (separate!) private jets to Washington to beg Congress for money to bail them out, I think it's safe to say the problems inherent in their downfall lie somewhere just beneath the surface – and not on the other end of a government bailout.

So when it comes to solving our own problems or reaching our own goals, we should start within ourselves. Know this: Money, possessions, relationships or whatever else you want will not, let me repeat, **will not** solve your money, possessions, relationship or other problems. The reason they won't solve your problems is because they are not your *real* problem.

Let's say you have a leak in your gas tank. Would putting more gas in your gas tank solve your problem? Well, maybe for a little while. But to really solve the long-range issue of a leaking gas tank we would need to ***fix the leak***. And that is where we need to begin.

Somewhere you've got a leak, and I can promise you it's in your mind. Until we fix it, no amount of money or anything else will make a difference. This not only applies to building wealth or furthering your career, but to every other area of your life as well. Whether you're trying to lose weight, or whether you're an athlete, a businessperson, or an actor, the concept is the same: fix the internal issue, and the desired external result will follow. We've all heard an ounce of prevention is worth a pound of cure.

Well, I think an ounce of root is worth a pound of fruit.

Thoughts Are the Origin of All Action

The only way to reverse circumstances is to reverse the ***cause of the circumstances***. As I will emphasize throughout this book, the cause of your circumstances is always related to your thoughts, so when you reverse the thoughts, the circumstances will follow. Look around. Everything you see that God did not create was created by man, and everything created by man was first conceived in the mind of man. This conceiving in the mind is known as *thought*.

I've heard it said that 70 percent of the success behind the winning car in a NASCAR event is the driver. Whatever the true percentage is, we certainly know the driver of the car plays a big part in the outcome of the race. Likewise, when the race of life starts we are born with a body, a spirit and a mind… and we are, of course, also the (earthly) driver. In Chapter 4, we discussed that we clearly have a spirit, a force of energy within us. In this chapter we'll to go a little deeper and examine how that inner spirit determines our outer lives.

If the Engine Makes the Car Go, then What Makes the Engine Go?

Let me ask you a question to start our deeper discussion properly. If the engine makes the car go, then **what makes the engine go?** Just like our mental world affects our physical world, the engine (the inside) plays a big part in how a car runs on the outside.

In other words, we know our inner world creates our outer world, but what creates our inner world? By becoming more aware of how the inner workings function, you will gain a better measure of control and guidance over the true root of the body's power: **the mind**.

You are already on the road of life; there's no turning back now. What you want is a better life, a smoother road, better rest stops and a more magnificent destination. Well, me too. My goal in this chapter is to give you better directions for getting where you want to go – and better gas mileage along the way.

Discover "The Recipe for Creation"

What makes up the "internal engine" of your mind? The mind is a very complex and fascinating concept and scientists will study it until the end of time. But remember, I want to keep things simple.

Let's look at what I like to call a mental recipe for creating whatever you desire. If you want a particular thing in your life then it's probably safe to say you don't have it (how's that for simple)! If you don't have it, then you need to create it. The following recipe can be used to "cook to order" any goal, desire or dream you have. See, we have all kinds of recipes for creating things in the kitchen, but we don't have near enough for our mind. And why not?

The fact is, just like there is a recipe to cook any meal on this planet, there is a recipe to create anything we want in life. The problem is that we never take the time to learn the right recipe. Too often we just throw the mental ingredients of our thoughts together and hope it turns out right.

We all know what usually happens when we don't follow the recipe in the kitchen. Sure, one out of every one-hundred times we wind up with something magical, surprising and delicious. But what about those other 99 times? Often we've wasted valuable time, money and energy on creating dishes that go straight down the drain.

Let's face it; all of our goals, dreams and desires are simply results we want to create. The question then becomes: What creates results? Variations of this formula are used by different teachers and I learned the formula I like to use from Bob Proctor and Harv Eker. It is aimed at giving you a better understanding of how your mind works. For the purpose of this book we'll call it the "*recipe for creation*."

In its simplest description, we can determine that the words and word pictures we use make up our thoughts. Our thoughts determine our feelings and emotions. Those feelings and emotions create our actions and our actions ultimately determine our results. Now, is it possible to dissect this formula with a fine-toothed comb and complicate it? Yes. Are we going to? No!

Remember, we're keeping it simple:

Words → Thoughts → Feelings → Actions → Results

Words Have Power (And Are Essential Ingredients)

To create a recipe for your better life, let's begin with words.

Many people overlook the importance of words. However, in Hebrews 1:3 we read, "God sustains all things by His powerful word." If God holds the universe together by His word, then is it possible that we may hold a little bit of our world together with ours? Additionally, we can't examine the impact of words without examining the instrument that speaks them. In the Bible it says that life and death are in the power of the tongue. Well, I believe it. I also believe that poverty and wealth are in the power of the tongue. As well as wisdom and ignorance, love and hate, etc. So let's not take our words lightly. After all, our words are the foundation of our thoughts, and we know how important foundations are, right?

In James 3, we read that even though a ship may be quite large and driven by strong winds, it is steered wherever the pilot wants to go *by a very small rudder*. It then says that, likewise, the tongue is a small part of the body but it makes great boasts. We're also reminded that a forest is set on fire by a small spark. In the same way, our tongues (which ultimately speak our words) have great command over our lives.

Words can do much more than impart meaning or give direction; they impact our very lives and, in many cases, our health. According to Patrick B. Massey MD, PhD, medical director of complementary and alternative medicine for the Alexian Brothers Hospital Network, "One of the most powerful healing tools we have are the everyday words we use. Their meanings and vibrations of their sound impart a profound and measurable effect on our health and the health of others."

When using positive words, we create a positive impact. When using negative words, particularly when it comes to our lives, situations, talents and abilities, we create a decidedly negative atmosphere. Can you imagine what this powerful ingredient can do when used incorrectly (negatively) in our *recipe for creation*? It can be like putting in salt when the recipe calls for sugar!

Throughout history, words have caused great and lasting change. When President John F. Kennedy challenged an entire nation to "Ask not what your country can do for you," he signaled a new era in industry, volunteerism and social and moral responsibility.

Martin Luther King's "I Have a Dream" speech breathed new life into the Civil Rights movement during the 60's and is considered one of the greatest and most notable speeches in human history. Through the use of his words, King was able to educate, inspire and inform the people not just on the steps of the Lincoln Memorial but throughout America and for generations.

And who isn't familiar with the three simple words – "Just Do It" – that helped build an empire? Who would have thought three words could be so powerful and create so much?

> *"We are masters of the unsaid words,*
> *but slaves of those we let slip out."*
> ~ **Winston Churchill**

Of course, we've also seen the negative effect words can have. In 2003, the country group known as The Dixie Chicks suffered a backlash when they announced they were embarrassed because U.S. President George Bush was from their home state of Texas.

Scores of fans turned against them and some even organized events where people destroyed Dixie Chicks CDs and memorabilia. Radio stations also stopped playing their music. They seem to have recovered from that controversy, but it's a perfect example of the power and consequences – both positive and negative – held in words.

I don't want to belabor the point, but I also don't dare take a chance of you missing it. So here is one more example that should scare the hell out of you so you always think before you speak.

In 1997, professional golfer Fuzzy Zoeller's remarks stirred up more debris than a hurricane through a junkyard. Zoeller finished his round and was asked to comment on Tiger Woods, who was on his way to his first Master's win. He began with kind words, but Zoeller's final remarks caused quite a controversy. He advised the press, "You know what you guys do when he gets in here? You pat him on the back and say congratulations and enjoy it and tell him not to serve fried chicken next year. Got it?" As he left, Zoeller added, "Or collard greens or whatever the hell they serve."

Now, I am one of the biggest jokesters you could ever hope to meet, so I have much sympathy for the consequences of these comments. Not just for Fuzzy, but for all involved, including the public and especially Tiger Woods. I myself have been misunderstood when I truly meant nothing bad, so I know how it feels.

My point in relating this unfortunate incident is despite the fact that Zoeller is a known jokester who publicly apologized and indicated he meant nothing hurtful by his "joke," his words still had major repercussions. In fact, his sponsor dropped him and the media had a field day. Those few sentences have been the focus of countless interviews and commentary and even 10 years after the incident, coverage of the 2009 Masters included a special segment about it.

The good news is that we can choose our words. Choose carefully.

Thoughts Stir the Pot (And Give Life to Words)

Now, let's focus on the power of *thoughts*. Our thoughts have extreme power, which should come as no surprise when we learn that scientists estimate we have 12,000 to 60,000 thoughts per day!

According to George Dvorsky, writing on behalf of the Institute for Ethics and Emerging Technologies (IEET), "A number of years ago the NSF (National Science Foundation) estimated that our brains produce as many as 12,000 to 50,000 thoughts per day depending on how 'deep' a thinker you are (other estimates run as high as 60,000 per day or more)."

Stephen Knapp, author of *The Key to Real Happiness*, adds, "In the course of our lives we may be bombarded with negative thoughts, energies or scenarios that may come not only from within us but also from outside ourselves or from others."

Dvorsky concludes, "Some people have estimated that upwards of 70 to 80 % of our daily thoughts are negative." Just imagine the tremendous impact of all those negative thoughts as you strive to achieve your goals. Every time you think "yes," your mind screams not just "no" – but "No, no, no! A thousand times no!"

There is no shortage of books and articles about thoughts, in the Bible or anywhere else. But one particular scripture really resonates with me and supports the foundation I laid earlier. It is Romans 12:2, "Do not conform any longer to the pattern of this world but be transformed by the renewing of your mind."

What this scripture clearly tells us is that if we want **transformation,** then we need to **renew our minds.** It doesn't say "If you want transformation, then you need to use the Law of Attraction." God knew that external change is made by changing the thing that creates it, and that is primarily our thoughts.

In the final analysis I think we vastly overcomplicate success, prosperity, accomplishment, contribution or whatever we desire. Regardless of your religious persuasion, let's examine something for a moment and see what you conclude: God supplied His people with a primary resource in which to guide our lives.

What was it? It was a book.

A book that is full of **words** and **thoughts.**

Don't you find that... *interesting*? If the God of the universe only left His people words and thoughts, then I conclude those words and thoughts are not just *somewhat critical* to a successful life. They're much more than that – they are **absolutely essential.** In fact, we read in Matthew 4:4, "Man does not live on bread alone but on every word that comes from the mouth of God."

My conclusion is that God knows exactly how He wired our brains and all we need to do is follow the instructions. We've all heard the words "when all else fails, read the directions." I am living proof that by following them first (instead of a last resort), things work out much better. Why? Well, if we think and act in accordance to the "Instructions," then we will be programming our minds at the root, which will make things in our outer world (our fruit) follow suit. See, God knew our thought life, wisdom and internal world would ultimately create our outer world.

Therefore, God left us with His words and thoughts, knowing they would produce the results we wanted – *if* we applied them. Many of us, however, either don't know what's in that instruction book and/or underestimate its power and purpose. We spin our wheels trying to get the outside world to cooperate with us while either neglecting or completely ignoring our inner world.

Maybe we hope that if we throw enough "stuff" at it, the problem will go away. Perhaps we think that if we ignore the problem, it will somehow magically fix itself. But no matter how much gas we pour in, if we don't take time to fix the tank, it's still going to leak; it's not going to go away, and it won't fix itself. And over the long haul, it's much more costly to try to handle things this way.

Whether you gain wisdom from scripture or from books that teach essentially the same principles I have found that there is not one area of life that God does not address in the Bible. I started out reading Proverbs because it had so much wisdom about business and life.

Affirmations? Or Nullifications?

Affirmations have long been a substantial ingredient in many recipes for personal development. They've been recommended in many of the personal development books I've read. I am not an expert on affirmations and there are many good teachers who can offer much more on this topic. For the purposes of this chapter, however, I'm going to explain why I believe affirmations work great for some and maybe not so great for others. If you are new to affirmations I encourage you to give them a serious try.

To begin, let's take what we've already discussed and agree that words and thoughts have real creative power. Our words have the power to create. When you affirm something, you are organizing, focusing and channeling thought energy, and activating known and unknown principles that begin making your affirmation a reality.

Personally, I struggled with affirmations in the past. However, I've had seasons in my life where affirmations really resonated with me and produced results. Other times I haven't been able to conjure up anything that produced belief, power or emotion. I'll never forget my first experiments with them. I read *Think and Grow Rich* many years ago and followed the exercise described in the early chapters of the book. I followed it every day, over and over. After about 90 days, I still wasn't earning millions of dollars, so I decided to stop doing the exercise.

Deep down I knew what I was saying to myself was not true and my affirmations didn't have any real power. The more I studied the mind, the more I realized why affirmations were not working for *me*. It's not that affirmations don't work. But the affirmation itself doesn't matter as much as what *you believe* about the affirmation. So, if you find affirmations work for you, then use them. If not, don't beat yourself up about not using them.

Different things work differently for different people. I have seen athletes go through some very interesting rituals to put themselves in a certain state of mind. In my affirmation practices, I said, "I am a millionaire," when I was absolutely broke. My mind said, "You are an idiot."

What I found to be much better to use was what I call a general affirmation. Here's an example I developed through my studies: "My life is improving every day, I am advancing, progressing and getting wealthier every day." Unlike the "millionaire" affirmation, I could actually *believe* this statement because it didn't have an exact dollar amount, address or deadline attached to it.

I concluded that if I simply got out of bed and engaged in life, I'd learn something. If I read a book for five minutes or listened to an audio program, I would learn something. If I learned something, then my life *was* advancing and progressing. As far as wealth was concerned, I simply modified my definition of wealth to make the affirmation more general and, therefore, more meaningful.

Suddenly real "wealth" meant more than money, but included spiritual, mental, emotional and interpersonal wealth. By repeating this affirmation over and over, I got excited. I wanted to read books and work on myself and do what I needed to do to accomplish my goals. I became highly inspired because I knew I was advancing, progressing and getting wealthier everyday.

As I've said, the biggest key to an affirmation is not the words you say, but whether you can *believe* what you say. Additionally, I believe affirmations need to be modified and adjusted along the way. Just as you wouldn't work out with the same amount of weights forever if your goal was to build muscle mass, you shouldn't affirm the same thoughts forever if you wish to "grow" in other areas of your life.

In Part 2 of this book I will outline examples in the Success Compass System that give you an opportunity to implement affirmations if you wish. In the meantime, I think the biggest thing you need to pay attention to is the conversation you have with yourself every day. If you say any of the following to yourself, then you're also setting in motion the forces to make it a reality:

- "I can't afford it."

- "I'm stressed."

- "I'm confused."

- "I'm overwhelmed."

- "That person is driving me crazy."

- "I'm tired."

- "I'm busy."

- "Things are crazy."

- "I can't."

- "It's hopeless."

- And on and on...

With these words recorded on your subconscious mind, it will go to work to validate them. This concept works for good or bad, positive or negative. It's why the rich get richer and the poor get poorer. It's why the busy get busier and the confused get more confused. And it's why YOU, someone who is already successful, will become even more successful.

I believe affirmations are to personal achievement what salt is to a meal. It will enhance the flavor of your food (experience), but it is not the whole meal (achievement). You need all the other ingredients as well. I like to think of affirmations as guard rails for my thoughts. They are always trying to run off the road and by affirming what I want to be, what I want to do and I what I want to have, these affirmations are keeping my thought life between the lines.

Your mind is going to carry on a conversation all day anyway. You may as well direct it toward your best possible benefit. The best way to combat any habit you may have of using negative or disempowering words and thoughts is to be aware and pay attention to what you think and say. If you catch yourself saying, "I am so busy," then change it to something like, "I am highly productive and this extra work I've chosen to immerse myself in is already paying off." This is called *reframing*. By reframing your words, you will create a different picture!

Now let's talk about the link between the affirmation and the action, the blueprint and the building, the thought and the thing, the invisible and the visible. For if words and thoughts are the ingredients, then action is the fire that sears them together to create that which we all crave: results.

> *"Expression is the dress of thought."*
> **~ Alexander Pope**

Many come to the table of the Law of Attraction ready to eat, but bearing no covered dish, no home-baked pie, no store-bought dessert or even a fork or napkin. If there is a trap of any kind in the teachings about the Law of Attraction, it is one that says you do not need to take action. As we read in Proverbs 28:19: "He who works his land will have abundant food, but the one who chases fantasies will have his fill of poverty."

The words of Henry David Thoreau also resonate with me. "If you have built castles in the air, your work need not be lost, that is where they should be. Now, put foundations under them."

By now, I think we all recognize that words and thoughts are like black music notes on a white page; inert and neutral until some force of will is applied. Action is that force of will. I hope I don't need to make a big case for the importance of action. Instead, I would rather discuss some perspectives about action that helped me create results in my own life.

I used to spend a lot of time sitting still and asking God what He wanted me to do. I spent so much time trying to figure it out that I never actually did anything. Based on some of the books I'd read, I thought I should be on top of a mountain for a month – just meditating. What I ultimately learned is that not doing anything is more exhausting then doing everything.

I heard the following words in a sermon once, and they immediately inspired me to take action: "God will show me where He wants me to go, but He can't steer a parked car."

I was caught up in taking the "perfect" action or the "perfect" step or making the "right" decision. If things didn't seem just right, I didn't do anything. Finally I began moving and discovered that if I *did* make a wrong turn, I'd find out pretty quickly and, instead of sitting there fretting about it, I could just turn around. The Bible says to "Be still and know that I am God." it doesn't say to "Know God and be still."

Right way or wrong way, U-turn or fast lane, at least I was moving. Furthermore, if you are relying on spiritual guidance then you also need to expect some *positive* spiritual roadblocks and detours that will lead you to where you should be going if, by chance, you're not paying attention to the road signs!

Now, what I'm going to say next may sound a little (maybe even a lot) materialistic, but it is something I had to work through so I'm going to share it anyway. It used to confuse me and make me angry when I saw a big junky car with a "Trust Jesus" bumper sticker. I'd think, "If that's the car I have to drive because I trust Jesus, then no thanks!" Of course, I have matured and grown a lot since those days. Fortunately, I've discovered where a lot of people make misinterpretations, and I think the subject of action is one of them.

I know a lot of people misinterpret "trusting God," and think they can just sit in the back seat and relax while God starts the car, pushes the gas pedal and drives them directly where they want to go. I have news for those people: God is not your chauffer!

Most of the time, we must step out in faith because, after all, if we could handle everything on our own, then we wouldn't need God. Exodus 14:13 gives an example of one man's faith... and God's response. Moses, in response to the frightened words of his people as they confronted Pharaoh's army, turned to his people and said, "Do not be afraid. Stand firm and you will see the deliverance the Lord will bring you today. The Lord will fight for you; you need only to be still." Guess what God said next? "Behold, use the Law of Attraction and you will be rescued?" NOT. He said, "Get Moving!"

God was ready to work miracles, but he needed His people to take a step.

"We're not necessarily doubting that God will do the best for us; we are wondering how painful the best will turn out to be."
~C.S. Lewis

I'll admit I've struggled all my life trying to know if I'm doing God's will. I've had more anxiety about this topic than any other. I used to ask God every day, "God, what is Your will for me?" and "God, do You really want me to do this or would You rather I do that?" Or sometimes, "God, is it Your will that I am in this spot right here, right now, doing this work?" I used to fret over this stuff big time. In the process, I wore myself out and just about drove myself crazy.

As a salesperson and a business owner I thought surely God had something more important and exciting in mind for me since I was ready to do His will. So I prayed and prayed, and then finally God showed me – I had the formula backward. He revealed that if I'd truly accepted His call and wanted to do His will, then *the work I did* was far less important than *how I did my work.*

Now, before I go on, I want to add that I believe some people are called to specific ministries and to serve as pastors, nurses, politicians, soldiers, firefighters, etc. But not all of us.

In fact, most of us don't need to get caught up – as I was – in asking, "God, is it Your will that I do this or that?"

That's not nearly as important as getting caught up in how we *behave* in this or that. Eventually, I understood the greatest thing going toward my results wasn't *the action I took* but *how I took the action.* It was about my attitude and heart while I did what I did purposefully as opposed to merely spinning my wheels and being active simply for the sake of being active. Furthermore, I learned that all jobs are important. There are many business people who don't belong in the pulpit and many people in the pulpit who don't belong in business. We are all given different strengths and talents for the purpose of serving others.

The subject of action/service can't be summed up much clearer than with these words, "Whoever wants to become great among you must be your servant, and whoever wants to be first must be slave of all. For even the Son of Man did not come to be served, but to serve, and to give His life as a ransom for many."

Let's begin to wrap this section up with an illustration. Think about a big, beautiful building or hotel. Before it was ever constructed, there was a big vision and a big blueprint. When architects created the model to show investors or renters, it was a modern sculpture with fountains, mirrored glass, carefully manicured lawns, plenty of parking and maybe a few of the latest architectural embellishments thrown in for good measure. But we all know where they had to go to make it happen. They had to go to the very bottom in the dirt and mud. Now, of course, the end result is always a beautiful and wonderful accomplishment. But that end result is only a one-day event.

In order to complete the goal portrayed in the architects' model, workers spent countless days laying one brick at a time and doing the basic labor with plenty of unruly concrete to pour and a fair share of lifting and toting and barely seeing any progress at all. Week in and week out, the work had to be done. Eventually, some progress was made that caused by passers to stop and remark, "What a beautiful building that's becoming..."

And this is basically what I've reconciled myself to understanding: it's okay to have a big vision with fancy blueprints, insignia, flowing waterfalls and St. Augustine grass as long as I never forget I am simply a brick layer and most days will look pretty much the same. And as we will explore in the Success Compass, once you complete a "construction" project your greatest need is to be engaged in another one anyway.

And finally I love the way Og Mandino puts it in *The Greatest Success in the World*. As we part with Chapter 5, here are a few of my favorite words from that book's "First Commandment of Success":

Work is not your enemy, but your friend. If all manners of labor were forbidden to thee you would fall to your knees and beg an early death. You need not love the tasks you do. Even kings dream of other occupations. Yet you must work and it is how you do, not what you do, that determines the course of your life. No man who is careless with his hammer will ever build a palace. Know that there is only one certain method of attaining success and that is through hard work. If you are unwilling to pay this price for distinction, be prepared for a lifetime of mediocrity and poverty. Always do your best. What you plant now, you will harvest later.

Thanks, Og. Those are some directions we can live with!

Review

The Success Compass system in Part 2 will give you a more thorough opportunity to apply the principles in this chapter. For now let's review the key points:

- We have a serious responsibility and a significant role in creating our lives.

- Watch your words!

- Most people try to solve problems from the wrong end. Fix the leak.

- An ounce of root is worth a pound of fruit.

- The only way to reverse circumstances is to reverse the cause.

Recipe for Creation

Words → Thoughts → Feelings → Actions → Results

So how can we apply the recipe for creation right now? Very simple, close your eyes and begin to think about what you want to accomplish and who you want to become. How do you act, walk and talk? Dwell on it. Think about it, smile about it, play it in color in your mind. See yourself doing and becoming everything you want. The very act of doing this is organizing your **words** and **thoughts**. When you have aligned the most desirable thoughts with what you really want to accomplish you will create a feeling of joy, passion, enthusiasm and energy, also known as **emotion**. This positive emotion will drive you to **action**. The action you take may be research. It may be reading a book, going to a seminar, etc., but there will likely be some information gathering. It will then lead to phone calls, meetings, presentations and actions of all kinds. And it will most certainly lead to **results**!

6

YOU CAN'T PUSH THE GAS WITH YOUR FOOT ON THE BRAKE

"Never tell me the sky's the limit when there are footprints on the moon."
~ Unknown

On a sunny day in Tucson, Arizona, a popular radio announcer told his listeners he had important news. He began ominously with, "At five-thirty this afternoon, two planets will align at just the position which will cause the earth to lose its gravitational pull." He continued, "If you jump into the air at this time, you will actually float for a couple of seconds."

Then the announcer took calls from listeners who shared their amazing experiences. One lady said she lifted her rear-end off the seat while she was driving and felt herself floating. Caller after caller told their stories. That is, until the DJ laughed and said, "April Fool's Day!"

This story is true, and while it's funny, there's also a powerful lesson to extract. Most everyone agrees that our beliefs are very important. However, I don't think people respect the *real* power of our beliefs. I think the power of belief gets watered down – much like goal-setting and the importance of having a positive attitude – because we've heard about it so much that, frankly, it has become "par for the course."

My goal in this chapter is to examine some new and different perspectives about beliefs. In the story above, people actually believed the earth had lost its gravitational pull. Therefore they really thought they were floating for a few seconds. What kind of beliefs can you program that will allow you to float to your goals? Mark 9:24 says, "I believe; help me with my unbelief." In Matthew 9:29 it says, "according to your faith it will be done unto you."

It sounds to me like belief (as well as faith) plays a very big part in our lives. At least a big enough part that we are told that in order to inherit eternal life, all we have to do is simply believe. If belief will get me eternal life after I'm dead, then what will it get me while I am alive?

Because of my feelings about the importance of beliefs, I consider this to be one of the most important topics in this book – not to mention our lives. Mastering the concepts in this chapter may be more significant to your success than all the others combined.

If you can master your beliefs, you can master your life. Why? Your beliefs are to your thought life as flour is to a cake.

There are other important ingredients such as sugar and cocoa or vanilla extract etc. But if you left out the flour, all the other stuff wouldn't mean much because your cake would never bake!

If you're going to change anything in your life, then changing your beliefs is paramount. Your beliefs dictate most of your thoughts, actions and reactions. They also influence your emotions and how you feel about what happens – or doesn't happen – in your life.

Imagine you went to the doctor and they took an X-ray and found a deadly tumor. You would certainly take drastic measures to have it removed wouldn't your? I think we must treat negative thoughts and disempowering beliefs the same way. As you increase your awareness and refine your personal philosophy, deadly beliefs will be revealed. Don't put a band aid on them. Destroy them! This is the attitude we need to have about beliefs.

If you can master your beliefs, then just wait – everything else will fall into place. The topic of belief has always been a principle in any religion or self-improvement teaching. *How and why* belief works is a mystery we will never understand. However, this chapter will help clarify what we do understand.

Believing is a Skill

You'll find many definitions of the word "belief" in the dictionary. However, not once is it referred to as a skill, and yet it's one of the most important *skills* you can develop. It's an area where you can make a substantially positive difference in your quest to move to a new level.

I recently watched an interview of Olympic champion Michael Phelps. He said a few things that shocked me. He said that when he's training, he consumes between eight thousand to ten thousand calories every day. He also said that in training for the most recent Olympics, he didn't take a day off for five years! As the interview ended, he said he'd begin training for the 2012 Olympics in January 2009, three years in advance of the actual event. The story gave me a different way of looking at things when I thought about physical training as compared to mental training. It's clear that the work he did during training is what made Michael Phelps such a success when it was "show time."

This concept is related to and parallels everything we've discussed about how your inside world affects your outside world. So how are these concepts linked together? Look at Michael Phelps' inner world commitment to his outer world. Then look at yourself. What if you gave just *half* that dedication, *half* that commitment and *half* that effort to *your* inner world? And, more specifically, to your beliefs?

Do you think doing so would have a positive impact on your life? You bet it would! Are you working on your inner world? Could you work a little harder? Just as you can be physically weak, you can also be spiritually and mentally weak. This includes your "fitness level" as evidenced by your beliefs.

In life we label skills one of two ways: soft or hard. Soft skills are those "warm and fuzzy" attributes we feel will be there whether we exercise them or not. Faith, hope, charity, love, honor and belief are some prominent "soft skills." "Hard skills" are the daily activities we actively seek and process as truly skillful behavior, such as our work performance, gaining knowledge, and exercising our bodies and minds to achieve, succeed and profit in this competitive world.

If you want to truly benefit from the Law of Attraction, you need to move *belief* from the "soft skill" category to the "hard skill" category and treat it as such. In fact, I believe that by thinking about belief as a skill rather than an intangible, elusive, metaphysical or spiritual "warm and fuzzy" act, you can bring it down to your level.

Why has belief been made to seem so mysterious, difficult and elusive? Why is it placed on a pedestal, when it's something we actively desire and protect every day? Treat it as you would treat anything else. Just as you can improve your sales presentation, your communication skills, your writing skills, your people skills or whatever else you need to improve; you can also improve your believing skills. And since, according to our belief, it is done to us, I can't think of a better skill to cultivate or improve.

Let's compare the ability to believe with the ability to type. Let's say the quality of your belief is about the same as a person who "hunts and pecks" on a keyboard. You can type a letter or get out an email fairly well, but you aren't very fast or confident and you certainly wouldn't get above average results if you were measured for speed and accuracy. But you know that with practice, your typing speed and accuracy could improve.

The skill of belief can be viewed the same way. Your current belief level may be the equivalent of typing 25 or 35 words a minute – or more, but you can *always* improve. And that's the goal of this chapter: to increase your believing skills.

It's Time to Hit the Gym: The Belief Workout

How do you strengthen your beliefs? The same way you would strengthen anything else. You work out, improve your understanding and awareness and, of course, you **practice**. The problem is most individuals have never considered belief to be a skill and certainly haven't practiced it. By the time our basic beliefs are set (typically in our late teens or early twenties), we usually don't change them much. Therefore, we don't buy into others' beliefs easily and we feel threatened when our own beliefs are violated or contradicted.

Now, consider how long your own beliefs have been in place. You may have held the same basic beliefs for several decades. By the time you reach your fifties or are ready for retirement, you've held the same beliefs for forty or fifty years! So take it easy on yourself. If you've had a poor diet for 25 years and need to lose 35 pounds, it isn't going to happen overnight. You can change your beliefs faster than your waistline, but it's going to take some time depending on the "mental shape" you're in.

You can make positive change by examining your beliefs in all areas. But the best place to start is to take an inventory of what you believe about yourself and what's possible for your life. Further, you need to examine your beliefs about adversity, change and challenge.

It's important to know that wherever you are right now is where you **believed you could be**. If you want to move up, then you must **move up your beliefs**. If you want to change, then you must **change your beliefs**. It's just that simple. If you don't believe it, then that's where you need to start. You need to **believe in belief.**

The inspiring story of Roger Bannister exemplifies the power of belief. You may already know the story, but even if you do, the lesson is worth repeating. No one believed it was possible to run a mile in under four minutes. But in 1954, Roger Bannister proved it possible when he ran the mile in just 3 minutes, 59.4 seconds! Within a year of Roger breaking the barrier, 37 other runners broke the record too! The year after that, 300 runners did the same thing.

What happened? Was something in the water? Did someone invent a new type of running shoe the next year, making it possible for more than a dozen runners to break the four-minute mile barrier? Hardly! This story proves belief is beyond powerful – it transcends all logic and reason and allows us to create our own miracles.

These broken records clearly show that before you can accomplish something in the outside world, you must first hold a belief in your inside world. The runners who broke the record *after* Roger Bannister had the *ability* the whole time; they could have done it all along. However, they didn't have the *belief* the whole time. Once they were able to see it, they could believe it and then they achieved it. But our goal for this chapter is to show you how to believe it first, then you will achieve it and of course, see it.

How then can you "Bannisterize" all the areas of your life where you want to improve? How can you reach your goals – even beat your personal best – without waiting for someone to show up and run the four-minute mile first?

If You Can Believe Backward, Then You Can Believe Forward

You can begin strengthening your belief by realizing you already have the skill; *you've just been using it incorrectly*. Instead of waiting for and needing to see *proof* that something is possible, you are going to find proof yourself. The difference is you don't need to wait for someone to give you evidence.

You are going to go out and find it for yourself. I will give you an example toward the end of this chapter. For now you just need to realize that the best proof that you can do something lies in the fact that someone else has already done it.

And I'll let you in on a secret: you already know how to apply belief because you already know how to worry and you know how to doubt. Belief is just practicing those same processes **in reverse**. Essentially, doubt is belief pointed in the wrong direction. Think about a time you were really angry with someone. Or think about a time you were heartbroken or had a grave financial concern.

Now, *really* think about this for a moment. Try to recall anything and everything about the thoughts you had at the time (or might have right now) and notice how these thoughts attracted more thoughts that were similar in nature. They stacked up to build a case and ***establish a belief.***

I've seen this scenario play out in personal relationships many times. Have you ever thought someone didn't like you? As a result, you interpreted every move they made, every word they said and every gesture they projected as "suspicious." You just *knew* they were saying bad things about you and consequently you saw them differently and maybe even avoided them. Your belief – your perception – colored everything they did or said.

Now, have you ever done this and found what you believed about that person was absolutely false? And that the whole time you'd been obsessing about how much they hated you, they'd barely given you a thought, let alone hated you? I bet you have.

The problem (and the opportunity) is that your mind (both conscious and subconscious) will do everything to collect what it needs to support your belief and manifest it in your physical world.

You may think people don't like you while in reality, they really do (or they're just indifferent about you). But if you *think* they don't like you, then you have planted a seed and ultimately, they may not like you because your subconscious will assemble everything necessary for that to happen.

Whether your belief causes you to act a certain way, say certain things, take certain actions (or refrain from taking them) etc., your subconscious will ultimately arrange things so the person doesn't like you. Now, of course, you can do this (and anything else) in the other direction and get the opposite results. In football, an interception can be good or bad. It all depends on which side you're on. Keep your beliefs on *your side* and you'll always score a touchdown in life.

Believing Stronger

Since belief plays such a huge role in accomplishment, let's look at what plays a role in belief. I said earlier that dictionaries don't mention belief is a skill. Of course, dictionaries *do* provide several definitions that can be summarized with this statement: "A belief is the mental acceptance of and conviction in the truth, actuality or validity of something."

We all have many beliefs, and each belief has a different degree of strength or weakness. In the physical body, strength is attained through lifting weights or doing any type of exercises that increases resistance.

Well, strengthening your beliefs is no different. The only way you can strengthen a belief is by lifting heavier "weights" and the only way to do that is to step in there and get under them. See, the universe doesn't give you challenging circumstances just for the sake of unpleasant circumstances. It gives you challenging circumstances so you have to think and *believe* your way through the situation – that's lifting the heavy weights.

In other words, if you haven't reached a certain goal then you haven't believed it correctly or for long enough. And sometimes the only way the Universe can get you to stretch your beliefs is by changing your circumstances.

Sometimes we find ourselves in what we consider negative circumstances in our outside world so we can gain the necessary growth in our inside world to go about changing our outside world.

Are you still with me? In other words, our inside world affects our outside world, but our outside world also affects our inside world. I have also learned and believe that sometimes the universe does this for us and other times we do it for ourselves, consciously or not.

Let me give you an example of how I gained this unique perspective. Many years ago, I had a goal to get out of debt. I had about $60,000 in credit card debt and made a plan to get rid of it. Then I went on a mission. I was in commissioned sales and had opportunities to earn big paychecks. In no time at all, I was out of debt and moving in the other direction. In fact, I had saved more than $150,000 in cash within a few months. But then something happened. I started spending money.

I thought, "Heck, with this much money, I can finally do some nice home improvements. I can get a new car. I can go on a vacation and on and on and on…." Remember, my belief and subconscious was set to "get out of debt."

However, when I found myself out of debt, my subconscious didn't know what to do besides get me out of debt. Therefore it figured that it better get me back into debt so it could effectively do its job! Insane, I know. But this is an example of how our subconscious can arrange whatever we program. In this example I changed my outside world (by getting into debt) so it would harmonize with the beliefs and convictions I had. However, this is not a good example of how we want to use our power.

Here are a couple more examples. I know people who were desperately unhappy in their jobs and dreamed of going out on their own and starting a business. However, they were too scared to take the risk. Deep down they really wanted this to happen, so their subconscious minds found ways to make them behave in ways that would actually get them fired. Then they had no choice but to take the plunge and venture into business ownership – even though they'd been afraid to do so before.

Through careful reflection, I discovered what my subconscious mind did when things were going very well. I would be on a good run and enjoying success in everything I did. I would be earning plenty of money, having fun, and living with a good balance in life. And that was the problem. Again, my subconscious knew I wasn't reaching my potential and the only way to get the best from me was to give me the worst. And that's what happened. I believe God allowed unpleasant circumstances so I would hunger for knowledge, hunger for work, hunger for study, hunger for passion, focus, creativity and whatever I needed to get to a new level.

This "back into debt" theory also applies to folks who set a goal of "getting back into my teeny-weenie bikini." The minute you reach your goal weight, your body wants to gain weight so it can repeat its "success" all over again.

My belief and experience is that sometimes the universe will flat-out change everything to fire you up to the point where you'll have no choice but to make the changes you need to get where you want to go. We are not meant to plateau; we are not designed to stay still, comfortable, sublime or fat. We are designed for motion – body, mind and soul.

Think about it: when you sit still too long, your body gets restless, itchy. We get "ants in our pants" and yearn to get up and go somewhere. Our minds are the same way; the constant chatter in our heads, if we really pay attention and plug into it, is the constant motion of our souls begging to be acknowledged, strengthened, refined and educated. It is only when we sit still and neglect our growth that change is forced upon us by the outside world.

When we exercise physically, we push ourselves and tear our muscles down for the purpose of rebuilding and strengthening them to grow stronger. I believe God realizes this is how most of us grow spiritually, mentally and emotionally. And for most of us, it takes an external change by God to get us to "break down" internally so we can make improvements that are in our best interest when we may not otherwise take the initiative. That's why outside circumstances are sometimes just part of God's strategy for our lives.

In Case of Emergency, Use the Stairs

If you're a football fan, then you've certainly noticed that both the offense and defense call in different plays, depending on the circumstances. Well, it's my experience that we need "plays" in life as well.

Just as a football team has certain plays for certain circumstances, there are contingency plans for events that happen in the external world. For example, if a hurricane strikes, do this. If there's a fire, do that. And on and on. Likewise, you need contingency plans for what you will think and believe when certain things happen, especially the things most of the world labels as "disasters." The problem is most people don't have good (if any) contingency plans in place for disasters in their lives (metaphorically speaking), and they "die" in the tragedy as a result.

For example, what would it mean if you lost your business? What would it mean to your business if you lost a key client? If your current relationship, job or circumstances don't work out, how will you be impacted? It's essential to know what would happen if certain essential aspects of your life changed and then determine how you would respond, act and behave in advance by having some "plays" ready to go.

Just as proactive plays are drawn up in the locker room to be executed on the field, I think proactive responses should be drawn up in the locker room of your life so you're ready when disaster strikes. And not just ready with what to do, but ready with what to think and believe.

Jail Break

Every year in the Unites States, people go to prison for crimes they did not commit. These are innocent people who end up in prison based on the evidence presented against them. The actual number of people who are falsely imprisoned will never be known. Hundreds of innocent people have been exonerated of their charges based on DNA, scientific data or other forms of evidence.

It's certain that hundreds of others are still being held unjustly because they can't prove otherwise. I have the utmost empathy for people who are victims of this appalling epidemic. Through some combination of lies, misinterpretations, mistakes and being in the wrong place at the wrong time, their lives ended up in turmoil and their freedom was taken away.

In addition to the unfortunate circumstances described above, there are victims of a different type. Their "crime" is, in some ways, even worse. It's worse because they actually did commit it. These are the people who spend their lives in a prison of fear and doubt, a prison of their own making. They've locked themselves up and they hold the key the entire time… but don't even realize it. Or worse, they do realize it and have gotten so use to prison that they choose not to leave.

As you go through life, you're on trial almost every day. And in this daily trial you are the prosecutor, defendant, judge *and* jury. Whether it's a goal you want to reach, a partner you want to date, a size of pants you want to wear, a fear you want to overcome or a doubt that's holding you back, there's always a little voice inside your head (we'll call it "the prosecutor") trying to present evidence to prove its case.

Unfortunately, as we know from false convictions, the verdict doesn't always come down to whether something is true. It may be swayed by whether the prosecutor can convince the jury that it's true. Sometimes the prosecutor can present a mountain of evidence or present the evidence in such a way that the jury will accept it as true, even when it isn't. This is why you must guard your beliefs and any "evidence" that comes your way.

In a criminal trial, one of the attorneys may file a motion to move the trial to a different area. The request to move a trial isn't based on the climate and restaurants of the new location. It is based on *beliefs*. Attorneys make this request because one side knows the jury pool in the area where the crime took place has probably formed beliefs about the case. This, of course, could hinder the possibility of a fair and objective trial. If the legal system will move heaven and earth to relocate a trial, don't you think you need to file some motions yourself?

Often the "prosecutor," that little voice in your head constantly spewing negative self-talk, will try to color the evidence to achieve its own end. For example, if you're trying to lose 10 pounds, the persistent belief that you've always weighed this much might cause your prosecutor to say, "you'll never reach your goal" or "you're just not meant to be thin."

If you're going to change your beliefs, you must act as your own defense attorney. Otherwise, your prosecutor's negative self-talk will prevail if you accept that self-talk as truth. By defending your own beliefs, you can maintain the beliefs you need and change the ones you don't.

You should always look for evidence to support the case you want to make as part of your change process. Stop taking the prosecution at its word; question the negative self-talk, doubt, fear and irrational insecurity by defending yourself – your beliefs – at every turn. It's time to acquit yourself of the false evidence your little voice (prosecutor) is presenting.

Pull out the key, unlock the jail and walk out in freedom.

"Everything we hear is an opinion, not a fact.
Everything we see is a perspective, not the truth."
~ Marcus Aurelius

Let's take a look at some common areas we all struggle with from time to time. Your perspective is your unique view on life. I think we all know people with unique perspectives: the glass-is-half-full folks, the glass-is-half-empty people. There are those who have a positive outlook regardless of life's harshest conditions or infirmities, and those who curse God and the day they were born over the slightest triviality.

Amy Tan, bestselling author of *The Joy Luck Club*, said, "If you can't change your fate, change your attitude." She could have just as easily said, "Change your perspective."

Have you ever finished a great meal, a fine cup of coffee, a great conversation with an old friend, learned a bit of good or unexpected news, walked out on a sunny day and learned that your car wouldn't start? So you thought, "Big deal," called AAA and went back inside for a little dessert while you waited.

Then maybe months later you skipped lunch, had a rotten day at work, got chewed out by your boss, rejected by a suitor, popped a button on your pants, walked out into the rain at the end of the day to find out your car wouldn't start, cursed the stars, cussed the parking attendant, smashed your cell phone and had to call AAA from a phone booth three blocks away, crying into the receiver?

Now, the same event happened – a dead battery – but your reaction to that same event was markedly different. Why? Your perspective at the time of the event was different. One day everything was going great, so all the dead battery got was a shrug. Next time, all was wrong with the world so the dead battery became the source of all evil. Same event, different perspective.

I can't stress enough the importance of perspective when dealing with your beliefs. How you view the world, whether you're a positive or negative person, whether you're stressed or overly-influenced by factors beyond your control, has a direct influence on what you believe – and even how *strongly* you believe.

Perspective is closely related to perception and, as most of us know, perception is NOT reality. Perception is merely our idea of reality and what is true for us. My good friend Dan told me a story about his dad, who had been in the hospital. Now, Dan admitted his dad can be on the grumpy side and his dad would be the first to agree. After he was admitted, the nurses ran some tests on Dan's dad and filled out his charts. When they left, Dan's dad grabbed the chart. Written on the top were the letters "SOB."

Now, he realized that people sometimes viewed him as a little rough around the edges, but this made him angry. He called a couple of the nurses in and began his tirade. He said, "Why did you write that on my chart? Now the doctor is going to think I'm difficult and you didn't even give me a chance."

The nurses, understandably disturbed by the outburst, asked Dan's dad what he was talking about. As he pointed to the top of his chart, Dan's dad said, "Right there, you wrote that I am an SOB."

Then one of the nurses calmly replied, "Mr. Eugene, that stands for Shortness of Breath!"

The story is kind of funny, but there is a little deeper aspect to examine. Dan's dad must have perceived himself in such a way that would cause him to conclude what he did. Perception is important not only about how you see the world, but also how you see yourself.

Maybe perception *is* reality until we know anything different.

It's okay to misinterpret little things from time to time, but when it comes to life decisions, personal philosophy and achieving our goals, can we really afford to take that chance? What worked for me was to develop some well-planned ideas for looking at the same things in a totally different way. I once watched Wayne Dyer in one of his numerous appearances on PBS. His simple words, "When you change the way you look at things, the things you look at change," motivated me to start looking at all aspects of my life in a different way.

What I realized is that many of us have been on a mission to figure out how to turn thoughts into things. What made a world of difference for me was when I began learning how to turn things into thoughts.

That's right; we must also be able to turn things into thoughts.

Effective Perspectives

Many "things" are already around you and will continually show up (people, circumstances, opportunities, adversities, etc). A much more important job becomes deciding upon the thoughts you will have about those things life throws your way. That's why I developed a list of what I call Effective Perspectives.

Success

What is success? Ask 50 different people and you'll get 50 different responses. One of the first distinctions I experienced and learned came as a result of listening to Earl Nightingale's classic audio program, "Lead the Field." At the time, I had uncertain, unreasonable and simply untrue beliefs about success.

I thought success meant having a lot of money, an "important" position and a nice house or car. Soon, however, I learned that adopting a new definition of success would allow me to change how I thought and, consequently, change what I got. How? First, I changed my definition to reflect that of Earl's which said that "success is steady progression of a worthwhile goal."

This was one of my first breakthroughs as I studied success principles and one of the most important discoveries I made. It was the launching pad for my future achievements.

Living with this new definition allowed me to see myself and believe that I was successful right where I was. Of even more importance, it changed how I felt. I spent many unfulfilled years on the treadmill of life pursuing success, when I didn't even know what it was. By adjusting the definition so it worked for me instead of against me, my life changed forever. I immediately considered myself successful, and consequently I began to walk and talk and act like a successful person. My subconscious mind was also programmed for success, and it didn't know how to do anything else besides arrange positive and successful circumstances.

This one shift in how you define success may seem simple, but I encourage you to adopt it or something similar. Two of the biggest reasons people don't achieve success are: 1) they don't know what it is and 2) they struggle to keep a healthy self-esteem. By adopting the definition of success I am suggesting, it solves both problems at the same time. You immediately achieve "success" because you have now defined it, and your self-esteem goes up because you have achieved success. You then begin an upward journey of one success after another. And there is no such thing as failure with this definition.

Lastly, I made an additional distinction when Jim Rohn uttered the life-changing words, "Success is not something you pursue; it is something you attract by the person you become." I think those words have had more of an impact on my life than most others. It forever validated the importance of lifelong learning and personal development.

Strength vs. Weakness

I've always known I was weak in certain areas, and I let it limit me in a lot of ways. It was the reason I was going to have to settle for less, sacrifice who I wanted to become and probably never obtain all the things I wanted to be, do and have. That is until I learned a couple of new distinctions about weaknesses.

The first thing I learned came from John Maxwell, who said that if on a scale of 1 to 10, (1 meaning I was terrible at something and 10 meaning I was outstanding) I was a 4, then the best I could probably do was increase it to a 6 (which is still bad!). But, if I was a 7 at something, I could increase it to a 9 or 10 and that's what people pay for. I was excited that I could forget about my weaknesses and instead work on my strengths. Now be careful. I am not saying we should ignore our weaknesses. I am saying they do not need to limit us.

Many weaknesses can be upgraded to acceptable levels. In business, I found the best way to bridge most weaknesses is through other people on your team who are naturally strong in an area you are weak. And from a spiritual perspective I reconciled this issue with some help from the words in 2 Corinthians 12:7 in which Paul describes an apparent weakness he has to deal with.

He had a strong desire to have it removed. However, God did not remove it. Instead He replied, "My grace is sufficient for you, for my power is made perfect in weakness." Paul then reconciles and boasts in gladness for the weakness because he can rely on God and not himself. He concludes by stating a powerful and useful belief we should all adopt: "For when I am weak, then I am strong." In addition to those words, I leaned heavily on a statement I heard many years ago: "It doesn't matter how smart you are, it's how you are smart."

Money

No subject conjures up more debate than money. I will tell you this: if you desire to attain financial wealth, you will never achieve it if you believe there is virtue in poverty or if you have guilt about attaining financial success.

You may desire wealth, but if "beliefs" in your subconscious mind sabotage you, it doesn't matter what you desire. I've heard it said that the best way to help the poor is to not join them. If you have any guilt about accumulating a lot of money then donate it to charity! I could write a book on this subject alone, and I just might! But in the meantime, I'm going to pass on a quote that forever changed my life because it changed my belief. Yes, I went back and forth about whether or not it was "okay" to make money. But no more.

One Saturday afternoon, I was privileged to attend a presentation by the late Fred Smith, Christian leadership mentor and guru. Seated in a wheelchair after a dialysis treatment, he captivated those of us lucky enough to be part of that special day. He shared his wisdom and helped me reconcile the money issue once and for all.

He said, "Openly desiring money is honorable, so long as one seeks money as a means to noble accomplishment. Money is, and has forever been, a trustworthy servant or a tyrannical master. The individual must decide which it will be." There's nothing else to say about it! Thanks, Fred.

Consistency

A lot of people consider consistency a valuable attribute – and I agree. However, most people emphasize this more in the external world. Make those extra calls, work hard, be on time, etc. Consistency is just as important in our internal world, and especially as it applies to our beliefs. We need to believe about something just as intensely as we would apply fitness to our physical health.

Think about what would happen if you ate great for a week and then ate pizza and ice cream for another. Then think about what would happen if you worked out for a week and then smoked cigarettes and drank beer the next. Many people do this with their beliefs. They're essentially doing a workout on the treadmill and smoking a cigarette at the same time. They believe and are full of optimism one week and then become doubtful and negative the next.

Having a set of *consistent beliefs* is one of the most important skills you can develop. Otherwise, your goals will resemble what happens to people who intend to chop down a tree (goal). Most people put a handful of nicks in each tree in the forest of their lives and then abandon them, thus killing a lot of trees instead of chopping down a couple. If you added up all the nicks in all the dead trees in your life (things you have started and quit), you'd be shocked to see how much more you could have accomplished.

Balance

Living a life of balance is radically misunderstood. I think it was probably stated in early personal development books and seminars and seemed to make sense. However, if you take a closer look, you'll find that not much of life is very balanced and the very act of trying to balance all the imbalances can be the root of frustration, disappointment and fatigue. For example, a woman is pregnant for nine months.

Then it takes 18 years to get the kids out of the house (and it took five seconds to conceive). Now, tell me how that is balanced? We spend 12 to 18 years in school and then 40 to 60 working. Again, not very balanced. We work five days and get two days off, if we're lucky; again, just a *little* lopsided. I think my point is clear. Stop trying to balance your life and instead work with the seasons. You don't go swimming when it's snowing outside and a farmer doesn't go to Disneyland in the spring.

Men, do you have young children at home? A newborn, maybe? Try to tell your wife you don't want to feed the baby every four hours because you're "out of balance" and need to watch some football and have a beer. The only balance you may get out of that is five knuckles balanced between your eyes!

Parting Words from the Prosecutor and Defendant

Before ending this chapter, I'd like to share an exercise that has helped me when I've had trouble with "evidence" presented to me by either my own inner "prosecutor" or other people. It parallels some of what we talked about in this chapter. We have seen that whether someone is guilty or innocent doesn't have much to do with the truth. Instead, it has to do with the evidence presented.

Any time you're dealing with thoughts of fear, negativity, doubt, worry, etc., pull out a sheet of paper and cross-examine every witness the prosecutor calls. Remember, you are the judge and jury, so the only way you can "lose" a case is if you give up and stop presenting evidence. I do this exercise whenever I doubt something or need to strengthen my belief about anything. The example below is a condensed version of some of the thoughts I had to deal with when I decided to write a book:

Prosecutor:

- You aren't qualified to write a book

- You're not smart enough

- There's too much competition

- You're not famous

- Even if you did write it, someone else could do it better

- The economy is terrible

- It's too difficult

- It will take too long

- It's already been said

- You're not "holy" enough to write a book that references anything about being a Christian

- You don't have any experience

Defendant:

- I can get qualified

- I can learn what I need

- It's time for some new teachers

- Most authors don't become famous until after their books are published

- There is always someone below me and above me on the intelligence scale and so there is always someone I can help

- Look at the opportunity in a terrible economy, people need guidance out of it

- I can hire a coach

- What else am I doing?

- But not like I am going to say it

- Many of the books in the Bible were written by men who at one time were murderers and adulterers, fishermen and tax collectors

- Now would be a good time to start getting experience

I've found that if you look hard enough and think long enough, you can find evidence about anything (positive or negative). When I wonder if there is a market for a product, service or idea in one of my companies, I stop and consider a couple of things. For example, I saw a commercial one day for a "Snuggie," I'm sure you've seen it. It's one of the funniest (and cheesiest) commercials I've ever seen, but it doesn't matter what I think.

Somebody is buying that thing. In fact, a lot of people are. The USA today reported in January of 2009 that over 4 million of them have sold. My wife was watching the commercial and said (in a redneck sort of tone), "Back where I come from they call that a sweatshirt!" And just when I thought I had seen it all they came out with a Snuggie for pets! Good for them. I figure if there's a market for all the gadgets out there, then there is a market for things that actually add value to people's lives. There are many ways to serve ideas, just like eggs, which can be painted for Easter or eaten fried, scrambled, hard-boiled, deviled, etc. So, too, can ideas be served in a multiplicity of ways that some enjoy and others won't. The good news is there is no right or wrong answer. If the evidence you present is enough to convince *you,* then YOU win!

Og Mandino offers incredible advice in his classic, *The Greatest Salesman in the World*: "Failure will never overtake you if your determination to succeed is strong enough." And from what we've covered so far, you know if your belief is strong enough, your determination will never be weak.

So there you have it. We've discussed how your perception of the world literally colors your world and, in many cases, defines your reality. In this chapter we've seen many self-fulfilling prophecies come to life, as in what happens when you think someone hates you because the person looks at you funny, and eventually the person does hate you – all caused by your paranoia!

If you're not careful, if you don't practice effective perspectives or learn how to believe forward instead of backward, your life will become a self-fulfilling prophecy of doom, gloom and mistaken beliefs. Take your beliefs off that pedestal; dust them off, turn them over, examine them and then examine them some more. Beliefs are not a soft skill; they are a hard skill and you must learn to exercise and stretch your beliefs if you're going to live the life you deserve.

> *Many of us have been on a mission to figure out how to turn thoughts into things. What made a world of difference for me was when I began learning how to turn things into thoughts.*

Review

- Negative thoughts and disempowering beliefs must be removed much like a deadly tumor.

- Beliefs are to your thought life what flour is to a cake.

- Belief is a skill. And, like all skills, it can be practiced, exercised and improved.

- Doubt is simply belief in the wrong direction.

- Have contingency plans not only for what you will do, but also for what you will think.

- How effective are your perspectives?

- Stay out of jail… never believe the lies of the prosecutor and never stop looking for evidence.

PART
2
WHERE THE RUBBER HITS THE ROAD

THE SUCCESS COMPASS SYSTEM

Well, here we are at last! It's time to learn how to apply the amazingly simple but profoundly effective **Success Compass** to your everyday life. As I said earlier, different people define success in different ways. However, I have found that the path to achieving each persons own definition of success is very similar. And that is where the **Success Compass** comes in. The best part about this process is that it has just three simple steps:

1. Program

2. Drive

3. Arrive

To better illustrate the **Success Compass,** I would like to refer back to the GPS metaphor from the beginning of this book. Now, think about a GPS/Navigation device for a moment. If you have ever used one, you know that it is a very simple concept. You input/program your desired destination. You grab the wheel, push the gas and begin driving. You follow the directions that it provides you in a step by step format and then you ultimately arrive at your destination. I believe our journey through life, the pursuit of our goals, the mechanics of our mind and even our spiritual dependence can be viewed with many similarities. In reality there are many factors involved in attaining goals or driving a car from one place to another, but they can be summed up very simply:

- Decide on your destination;

- *Program* it in the GPS,

- *Drive* to where you are going and finally,

- *Arrive*.

This simple formula and metaphor can be used for accomplishing everything you want on your journey through life. It will help you organize your goals so you can pursue them with simplicity and consistency. How? Well that's what Part 2 of this book is all about. But here's a tip: I have found when you look at everything you want to accomplish through the lens of the Success Compass you can stay on track like never before. Anything and everything you do is a sequence of *Programming-Driving-Arriving*. When you stay very conscious of this you won't worry, fall into confusion and begin to doubt where you are going. But, before we go any further, I want to remind you and make sure you are clear on why there are two sections to this book.

See, many people will write and rewrite their goals every so often and especially at the beginning of the year, when we dress up our "Goals" and instead call them "Resolutions." You may attend seminars where they'll ask you to write down your dreams and goals and then decide if you want to accomplish them in one year, three years, five years, etc. This is a great practice, and I have benefited from it personally.

What took me to a whole new level, though, was changing my inside thinking before I re-set my goals again. And I hope you're on that same road now that you have finished the first part of this book. If you recall, back in Chapter 5 we agreed it would be silly to keep putting fuel in a leaky gas tank without first fixing the leak. Well, it would be equally silly to keep setting goals without fixing your thinking, beliefs and perspectives about yourself, how you create, what you believe and how God is working with you.

A good scripture to consider before you set any goal or program any destination is Ephesians 3:20: "God is able to do exceedingly abundantly above all that we ask or think." I don't know about you, but when I think about that I tend to set my goals a bit higher knowing that "Someone's" got my back!

When you set goals based on what you feel you can accomplish with your skills and your own power, you will never set them as high as you should. I've heard it said that God doesn't call the equipped, He equips the called. This belief has helped me to set goals based not on who I am, but rather based on who I can become while I am on the way to where I want to go.

By now we know that whoever sows sparingly will also reap sparingly. Well, whoever programs little arrives at little. Most people program a bonsai tree; how about a redwood? The Bible also says we have not because we ask not. I also like to say we have not because we program not.

If You Want a Better Destination, Get Better Directions!

A GPS exists, for the most part, to give you directions to a destination you program into it. If you don't program a destination, the GPS just shows you where you are. Well, your mind works pretty much the same way.

It can calculate the route to any destination you want, but it can't do its job if you don't first **program where you want it to take you**. Therefore, the starting point to all achievement, goals, a construction project or whatever you want to call it is a clear understanding of what you want. In fact, Napoleon Hill, the author of *Think and Grow Rich,* said a definite purpose is one of the most critical pre-requisites for success.

Remember, you're not making a decision to put the Law of Attraction into effect, it's always in effect. You do, however, want to learn how to use it for you instead of against you. You're learning to travel the road of life and drive better, faster and safer and get more miles per gallon on the road to your programmed destination.

One of the best things about a GPS is that you can be completely lost and have no idea where you are (or even where you're going), but if you simply decide upon and program a new destination, you can move away from where you are toward where you want to go. You'll no longer be lost! You can do this with your life as well. Jim Rohn said, "You can't change your destination overnight, but you can change your direction."

I think many people have become disillusioned by wrong turns and detours and have completely given up reprogramming their GPS to take them where they want to go. They don't truly realize it is only by taking the step of programming a new destination that they can begin to move toward it.

Part 2 of this book will get you back on track. It will fill your tires with air and get you where you want to go, and, get you there faster, safer and smarter. And, of course, since every trip starts with programming, so does Part 2.

7

PROGRAM

"If you don't know where you are going, you will probably end up somewhere else."
~ **Lawrence J. Peter**

If I had written this book 10 years ago, this chapter would have looked a lot different. I would have included a rigid goals section and demanded that you write them down and look at them every day. I would have said to be very specific about what you want and set a deadline for achieving them.

All these wonderful suggestions – and others like them – are excellent techniques when it relates to setting goals. But, if you're like me, you have done that before and it didn't always work. Or maybe even worse, it *did* work and you still felt empty. Before I continue and risk being misunderstood, let me say that I have the utmost respect for goal setting and I am constantly in the process of setting and achieving goals myself.

Research on the significance of setting goals is overwhelming, well-documented and convincing. However, along the path of my life's journey I have made some discoveries that allowed me to exercise more flexibility when it comes to setting goals. And speaking of flexibility, ask any athlete about its importance.

If you aren't flexible and you haven't stretched, then you risk injury, possibly a serious one. There's something to be said about that when evaluating the goals you want to set and the destinations you program into your GPS.

Don't Relax Your Pursuit of Goals; Relax HOW You Pursue Them

I loosened up on goal setting in the following manner: I didn't relax my pursuit of goals. Instead, I relaxed how I pursued them. I used to think that if I didn't write down that I wanted to earn one million dollars per year, live on Maple Street in San Diego by the time I was 30 and drive a red Ferrari, then I wouldn't accomplish it. Horse patootie!

This has been my hang-up with New Age philosophy from the beginning. It claims you attract everything, regardless of what you do or, for that matter, *don't* do. Well, I wonder if the little girl who was kidnapped was responsible for attracting that, or if the passengers in a plane crash attracted *that*.

I don't believe life can be real with you until you are real with life. In short, in life there are going to be detours; the only way to deal with them is to plan for them – and that includes being flexible with your goals.

Instead of setting a goal that may contain an exact address, city name or dollar amount, I have found it *much* more productive to set a direction. If I live in Texas and I want to change my destination, then I find it better to decide I am going to head out west, as opposed to saying I am going to go to XYZ Street in this exact neighborhood. Not only does this allow for detours along the way, it takes a lot of the stress out of the journey itself.

I don't know about you, but when they asked me in high school what I wanted to be in five years, I didn't have a clue. I didn't have a clue what I wanted to be doing in five hours, much less five years. How can we possibly make such an important decision in high school? It's hard enough to get this stuff straight before 40, and yet we beat ourselves up over it starting as teenagers.

I have found this to be the same as being asked about your life's purpose. Personally, I think our purpose is a moving target. I know my purpose has changed and evolved as I have changed and evolved – personally, professionally, spiritually and financially.

I don't believe in getting hung up on a purpose or a goal nearly as much as getting hung up on a direction. Why? When we set goals with no regard for the direction we're taking, we usually end with goals that take us in a direction we may not want to go. For example, when I was new to personal development and success principles, many of my "goals" were tangible things: a new car, a home, a mountain bike, a watch, etc.

Goals like this can strap us financially and keep us from going in the direction we really want to go. Considering the direction first allows us to make more mature, accurate and beneficial decisions. Furthermore, real satisfaction and fulfillment, which is what we all want, come from the direction we are moving much more than the goals we attain. Goals are important, but put them in the proper perspective. They serve as important mile markers that confirm we are traveling in the direction we intend to go.

This shift in perspective worked for me. I'd struggled for years with mission statements, goal setting, and trying to figure out my purpose in life. Casually and without much consideration for my direction or destination, let alone the journey, I set goals that seemed significant and worthwhile *at the time*.

It wasn't until I went through an exercise with a personal coach that I was able to take a mission statement of several hundred words and condense it to three. Those three words forever changed my life. Those three words were not a goal; they were a direction – and a purpose. When you decide on a direction, the goals you need to program will become obvious and you won't need to set them at all.

You will just accomplish them.

The three words from my exercise with the personal coach were: "Waking People Up."

That was the direction I wanted to go. The minute I reduced it to a simple direction, my subconscious gave me all the goals I needed to start working on. This book is a result of knowing that direction. I'd had a goal to write a book for more than 10 years, but never got started. Once I had a clear direction and purpose, to "Wake People Up," I wrote this book in about two years.

Is a Goal a Purpose or Is a Purpose a Goal?

Let's get a little more specific about this. Let's take a look at the difference between a goal and a purpose. By understanding how each is different, you can make the best decisions:

A **goal** is a precise, measurable outcome that you wish to attain; it has a specific beginning, middle and end. There is a point of accomplishment or attainment where you can put that check on a list.

In addition, goals have deadlines. That is one of the main distinctions between a goal and a purpose. Deadlines are important because when we don't commit to a deadline, we tend to procrastinate. What would happen if Christmas Day wasn't on a calendar? What would happen if you were told to just have Christmas every year when you could fit it in your schedule?

Can you image how messed up the holidays would be? Instead, a wonderful holiday happens every year because December 25 is a firm deadline on the calendar. You should do the same with your goals. Finally, the object is not to *go to* your goals, but rather for your goals to *take you* to your dreams or purpose.

A **purpose** is less specific. It may have intangible aspects to it and therefore is not always as easy to measure. It can be an ongoing and unfolding intention or desire. It will almost always encompass specific goals, but a purpose in and of itself has no end. It continues unless you modify it or decide to change it completely. The biggest indicator of a purpose is that it is tied to the service of others. If it does not serve others, then it is not actually a purpose and is simply a goal.

I think goal setting has gotten so much hoopla over the years that a lot of people no longer take it seriously. I think the main reason for this is most people don't really understand what they're doing when they set goals. As a result, they don't think goal setting is important.

If you simply think of setting goals (destinations) as programming your GPS, you may have a different perspective on the importance of goal-setting as a practice in your life. For instance, if you had to figure out how to navigate to a strange address in a big city, wouldn't you program the GPS? Would you say, "Oh, I know what my goal is, I don't need to write it down"? No way. The act of programming the destination is simple but critical to get "universal GPS of the mind" to calculate your route.

You should view goal setting in much the same way. If you are one of those people who never fills out worksheets or sets goals, that may tell you something about why you haven't reached some of your destinations by now. You're reading this book for a reason. You haven't arrived where you want to be or something in your life isn't going as you'd like. Surely, it can't be as simple as writing things down, can it?

Well, I won't say that it's *that* simple, but I will say it is *mandatory*. If you program a destination into your GPS, you still have to pay attention in traffic and you still have to stop at red lights and turn left when it's time. You still have to maintain your vehicle, change the oil and get regular tune-ups, etc. But the whole trip starts with programming the destination.

I like to think of it this way: you don't set goals because of how your mind works; but it's because of how your mind works that you set goals. Perhaps Zig Ziglar put it best when he said, "If you want to reach a goal, you must 'see the reaching' in your own mind before you actually arrive at your goal."

My mistake was setting goals **with no purpose**. Your purpose is the reason you set a goal in the first place. For instance, let's say you want to attract your ideal mate. *That* is your purpose. Within that purpose will be conditions you believe are necessary to accomplish it. One of those ideas may be to get into excellent physical condition. This will cause you to set specific goals in the areas of fitness. You may need to lose weight, gain muscle, get more exercise, etc.

So how will you get there? You set goals to achieve that purpose; goals may include, "I will take my lunch to work each day to avoid eating out," or "I will skip that bowl of ice cream after dinner except for the weekends," or "I will get up early and walk before work three days this week."

Once you know your purpose, you will unconsciously set goals to support your purpose, not the other way around. It is also recalling your purpose in the difficult times that will keep you pushing toward your goals when it may seem easier to just give up.

Here are Some Examples of a Purpose:

- To add value to others
- To wake people up
- To encourage people
- To lead others to spiritual maturity
- To be wealthy
- To advance the gospel
- To help the less fortunate
- To be healthy
- To be happy
- To feed the hungry

Here are Some Examples of Goals:

- **Finances:** To earn $100,000 a year; to become a millionaire; to retire by age 40

- **Physical Health:** To reduce my weight to 175; to lose 5 inches around my waist

- **Relationships:** To go on two dates a month with my spouse, to attend one social function every other week

- **Career:** To get promoted to sales manager in two years; to finish college; to go back to school

- **Spiritual:** To pray every day; to go to church every week

- **Possessions:** To buy a new home by the end of next year; to buy a black Lexus LS460

I realize this goal/purpose stuff can be a little tricky and is sometimes hard to tell the difference between the two. Let me give you a personal example to further clarify. One person could consider the writing of a book a purpose; another person could consider it a goal. It's not that one is right and another is wrong. Each person WILL have different purposes and goals for their lives. For me, as I stated earlier, my *purpose* was to "wake people up". The writing of my book is a *goal* that helps me to fulfill my purpose. My book had a finish line, a completion date and was measurable to achieve. My purpose is ongoing. Do you see the difference?

It takes time to reflect on what you really want. It takes careful thought to consider your purpose and your goals. It's not supposed to be that easy. But that is also why so many people struggle to achieve what they want and/or are unfilled when they do get what they want. So, if this seems a bit difficult then you are on the right track. But don't let the difficulty stop you from thinking through your purpose and goals. It's usually the very thing that makes the difference between real success… and real failure.

> *I like to think of it this way: you don't set goals because of how your mind works; but it's because of how your mind works that you set goals.*

Use Your Miles Wisely

Finally, let me drive home the importance of defining your purpose, deciding on your goals and then finally, ***programming*** them. Let's look at life as if you are a car and every day you have a choice of where you drive, how far you drive and even if you drive at all. That's right; you can still get where you're going even if you leave the car in the garage from time to time. The one thing you can't avoid, however, is putting miles on your car while you are driving. Remember, this is only a metaphor!

For our purposes, we will equate driving with working. Every day when you get up and go to work it puts miles on your car. Everyone has the same 24 hours in which to drive their cars. This is not the question. However, the question is where your accumulated miles will take you.

For instance, two cars can drive for five years and at the end of those years, both can have the same number of miles on them. But one car could have aimed at a distant and worthwhile destination and traveled to the other side of the world. Meanwhile, the other car could have driven aimlessly in circles around town and still be parked in the same driveway as five years ago.

In other words, use your miles wisely; make them count as much as possible. Start by deliberately aiming them in a direction you want to go. Abraham Lincoln said, "The best way to predict your future is to create it," and Programming, which is Part One of the Success Compass, does just that.

Once you've considered the ideas in this chapter, it's time to take the final and more tangible step of actually programming where you want to go. This means to write down your purpose, goals and/or desired destinations, type it up or key it in. Habakkuk 2:2 says, "Write the vision, and make it plain on tablets, that he may run who reads it." I'm sure if they'd had notebooks or computers in those days it would have said "type it" as well.

If you want to get a rock and chisel and be completely spiritual about setting your goals, then by all means go for it! But I think a pen and paper will do the trick. Writing down your goals is not a new idea and nobody can fully explain the power behind it. It's been said that it crystallizes your thinking and when you can see your goals on paper they become more real.

I've always believed this fundamental truth because a "published" goal is a **thought you can see**. And the more clearly you can see it, the faster you can achieve it. A thought in your head is intangible. It is real, to be sure, but it's still floating around in an invisible realm. Writing that thought down brings it into the most tangible form possible before it becomes the thing, the circumstance, you want. You make it more concrete by looking at your goal frequently.

That's all there is to it. It's not that hard. Just do it already! It doesn't take long to program a GPS in your car and it doesn't take long to write your goals down on paper, either. Just remember, a GPS won't go to work on the route to your destination until you go to work on the Programming.

Now, let's move on to the next chapter where we will grab hold of the steering wheel and put our foot on the gas…

Review

- Life can't be real with you until you are real with life.

- Determine your purpose, and then your purpose will determine your goals.

- A goal is specific and measurable and has an end.

- A purpose is less specific and is tied to the service of others and has no end (unless the purpose is changed).

- You don't set goals because of how your mind works, but it's because of how your mind works that you set goals.

- Where are your accumulated miles taking you?

8

DRIVE

"Even if you are on the right track, you will get run over if you just sit there."
~ Will Rogers

This chapter is not going to emphasize what action to take or how to take action. I am not going to cover how to organize your goals, how to do strategic planning or how to prioritize your activities. I'm going to assume that if you have made it this far, then you understand the importance of taking action and will brush up on the previously mentioned skills if needed. Instead, we are going to spend time evaluating one of the greatest principles I have learned: ***The best way to get where you're going is to be where you are.***

Since driving is 99 percent of the trip, we need to become good drivers. When you plant a seed in the ground, the longest part of the process is the growth in the middle. The drive to your goal will be similar. Therefore, we are not going to just *talk* about the importance of living in the present moment; **we are going to learn how to do it**.

The idea of living in the present is widely accepted as a great concept. The problem is that it's heard by many but practiced by few. However, one thing is sure: *You can't arrive anywhere if you don't show up when you get there.*

I think the number one reason people lack joy and contentment is because they fail to equip themselves with the perspectives necessary to help them place more value in the journey rather than the destination. And it should be of no surprise that tackling this issue starts in our mind.

Remember Fred Smith from our discussion in effective perspectives? Well, he shared some profound advice when it comes to this idea as well. Let's take a look at his excellent view on how we should see the world and the time we spend on this planet:

> *"When we feel that time is simply the 'entrance ramp' to eternity, it gives us a feeling of continuity. This life becomes the practice, and the next life becomes the game. Whichever we believe to be the game or the practice is extremely important, for so often we play this life as if it were the game, not understanding much of the drudgery and discipline of practice. When we understand life as the practice with the game coming later, we even accomplish some joy in the practice by anticipating the joy of the game."*

I was reminded of this living in the present and enjoying the journey principle last Easter. Have you ever seen kids on an Easter egg hunt? They are bursting with excitement as they look for eggs. They *know* the eggs are hidden somewhere and, of course, it's fun for them to find them. However, the looking is even more exciting. Don't believe me? Try this: Put 20 eggs in a basket on the coffee table and then tell the kids that's their Easter egg "hunt." They'll immediately say, "Hide them!" I believe that as adults, this looking, searching, striving is what we subconsciously want, too.

I see another example of this almost every day where I live. My home is on a lake and people fish there every day. There is not a "catch and release" law on our lake and yet every time they catch a fish they throw it back. (I am assuming I would do the same thing if I could ever catch anything.) I wonder why this happens. Could it be that the joy is not in the catching, but in the fishing itself?

"Do not take life too seriously. You will never get out of it alive."
~ Elbert Hubbard

I think another part of the problem is that we see so many results all around us that we become disillusioned about what it took to actually create them. We see a building but we never saw the planning, zoning, blueprint, building permits or construction crew. We never saw the financing details, the obstacles, the weather delays and the mistakes along the way.

We hear a number one song on the radio, but we don't know about the hours of work it took to craft the words, rehearse the music and produce the recording. We read a bestselling book and can't even imagine the number of hours of research and time spent in front of the computer.

We see Michael Jordan defy gravity and forget he was cut from the team in high school. We certainly have no clue as to the time and preparation it took to accomplish what he has achieved both on and off the court. I can guarantee you if we added up the hours Michael Jordan spent in games versus the time he spent in practice; the latter would be much higher.

And so it is with us and our "drive" to achieve our goals. We get easily frustrated because we think everyone else is already where they should be. We think five years on the corporate ladder or in our own business is more than enough time to get to the top, not realizing – or in some cases, not even caring – that those men and women who reached the top took three or four times that much time to achieve their goals. When we get frustrated, we aren't happy; and when we aren't happy we don't feel fulfilled. And when you aren't fulfilled you are usually pretty miserable.

Life Doesn't Start 10 Pounds, 10 Thousand Dollars or 10 Years from Now

The bottom line is this: if you're not happy where you are, you won't be happy somewhere else. If you're not happy with what you have **right now**, you won't be happy with more. If you don't live in the moment, when *will* you live?

Want proof? You've already passed a mile marker in your own life that you thought would make you happy and content. You've either made more money, achieved that goal, got that promotion, married that person, had that baby, bought that car, moved into that home and *have* obtained what you thought would make you happy and fulfilled when you got it. Ah, but here you are, reading this book, still searching for a way to find **happiness** and **fulfillment**. After attaining a couple of goals in life but still feeling empty, I decided I'd better get good at the stuff I am talking about in this chapter.

Happiness, contentment, accomplishment and the like don't come because you've suddenly reached a certain point in your life; they come through hard work and diligence, one day at a time. It's like the car you see speeding, cutting people off and running lights. Did the driver get there any faster than you did through all his crazy antics? Did he "beat" you? No. He drove like a lunatic and you were relaxed and stayed at the speed limit. Then you pulled up right next to him at a light, and he was more frustrated than ever.

When all was said and done, he didn't get there any faster and was stressed out in his attempt. What's worse, he stressed out the people around him in the process. Or maybe you're reading this and thinking, "Oh, man, *I'm* the crazy driver he's talking about!" I've heard it said: "There is no way to happiness, happiness *is* the way."

Great idea if you know how to do it. So let's keep learning.

> *"It's a mistake to look too far ahead.*
> *The chain of destiny can only be grasped one link at a time."*
> **~Winston Churchill**

Are you convinced that you do "live in the moment?" The fact is, most of us weave in and out of varying degrees of present moment living. A more important question is; do you *really* believe that true happiness and contentment come from living in the present? Have you tried this idea and found yourself struggling with responsibilities and the business of life to the point where you can hardly catch your breath to live in the present moment?

If that's the case, don't worry – you're in good company. It isn't easy to get into the habit of living in the present. It takes so long to achieve our goals, secure our dreams and become satisfied with who, and where we are that we constantly vacillate between satisfaction and dissatisfaction, anxiety and pure bliss.

The fact that you're struggling with living in the present versus "saving" your happiness for tomorrow is a big indicator you are on the right track. At least you're aware of it and are chopping away at it over time. The playoffs in any athletic competition bring tougher opponents as you try to advance to your goal. I believe mental and spiritual advancement is very similar. As you try to grow and become more, you also run into bigger and tougher obstacles.

Compare this to the person who doesn't know there's even a present moment to begin with; that life doesn't start 10 pounds, 10 thousand dollars or 10 years from now. Subscribing to that theory, they go through life only half awake. They function on autopilot with a mediocre life to show for it.

Whether you believe a near death experience is possible or not, it is well-documented that people who claim to have experienced them have a new outlook on life because they make a shift on a conscious and subconscious level. They declare they *know* there is an eternal side, and therefore they engage more fully in the present, which ironically gives them more of a future during their short stay on earth. So how can you improve your ability to live in the present and believe in the future... without having to almost die?!?

> *"We are always getting ready to live but never living."*
> ~ **Ralph Waldo Emerson**

What's the best way to live in the present? One way is to stop multi-tasking. Multi-tasking was a great solution to the way we lived at the end of the twentieth century, when 60-hour work weeks became the norm rather than the exception. And while being able to accomplish two or three things at work at the same time sounds ideal, it can lead to unhappiness and anxiety in life. Don't get me wrong, I believe in accomplishing a multitude of tasks, just not so much multi-tasking. Living in the present allows you to accomplish more, not less, and with better quality, not worse.

So in order to live in the present, to enjoy the moment, you need to leave multi-tasking back where it belongs – in the 90s! If you're on the phone, then close your computer and practice listening. It's a simple and effective equation you can apply to many circumstances in life. If you're reading and sending emails while you are on the phone, everybody is losing out, especially you. This one example may seem so trivial but it can be disastrous. I know first hand. I was on the phone one day (not being present-and certainly not listening). The person I was talking to gave me some very important instructions and I never heard them. When we hung up the phone they thought I was taking care of something urgent for them. Instead, I went back to my emails. The trivial detail (not!) was to change the date of a seminar I was setting up for them on the promotional material. I never did it! My lack of follow through caused a major hassle for both of us, people showed up when we didn't and vice versa, all because I was trying to save some time! Living in the present will save you more time than it will ever cost you.

Another way to see if you're in the present is to see if you're actually chewing your food. A majority of people could do more to affect their weight loss attempts if they would *be present* when they sat down to eat. I am guilty of this as well, but when you shove food into your mouth, it's simply because you are not present. You are not conscious and your mind is somewhere else. Life and food should be treated the same. We should smell it, touch it, taste it, digest it and let it nourish us rather than shoveling it in as fast as we can and missing the point entirely.

If you are with your kids, then be there; not just physically, as I've been guilty of, with a Blackberry in one hand and my kid in the other, but *without* the Blackberry; focus your eyes, ears, heart and head exclusively on that child. Even though a GPS unit knows where it's taking you, it only shows where you are. It knows how to be present and you should too.

Start Your Engines!

"In a day when you don't come across any problems you can be sure that you are traveling in a wrong path."
~ Swami Vivekananda

You programmed your destination. You have energy, enthusiasm and you are getting results. You're confident, living in the present and making swift progress toward your goal. You are excited and you say to yourself, "Hey, this stuff really works!"

But wait, what happened? All of a sudden, it seems things have blown up in your face. Yesterday you were on a roll. Today you face obstacle after obstacle. Things seem to be falling apart. What went wrong? When you program your goal and begin driving toward your destination, you start to make swift progress. However, you create an aspect of traveling that most people don't account for, and that is, you begin moving toward inevitable obstacles just as quickly.

Additionally, tedious details pounce on you and you think there must be a glitch in your GPS. "I didn't program this," you think. Now there are "pieces" lying around (circumstances, relationships, environment, etc.) that don't match up with the picture of the new destination you have programmed. These pieces are what's left of the old picture. You're also attracting new pieces and everything is blending together.

It is at this turning point where you have to make a decision. And the real decision is not whether to keep going or turn back. These will only be the outcomes of a greater decision. The real decision you must make is what you believe about what you are going through. The early stages of goal advancement can cause confusion and overwhelming anxiety. When this happens to you, remember to stay poised but most importantly *get excited*. It means you are on the right track.

Think about a puzzle for a minute. What is it really? Is it one picture? Or is it a bunch of small picture pieces? I say it's both. And your old life, the one you are leaving behind with each passing page, is made up of the same thing.

Your new life, the one you want to achieve, is no different. The problem, however, is this: you can change your picture in an instant but there are many, many pieces that make up the new picture and it will take time to assemble and put together. The dust will settle as the pieces of the old picture fall away and the new ones come into place. But remember, it's quite normal for some confusion and overwhelm to present itself when you have all the pieces for two different pictures laying around. As you begin to eliminate one and create another, the pieces will surely fall into place as long as you keep looking at the picture you want to put together.

Don't Pray for Lighter Burdens; Pray for a Stronger Back

There are many views on how hard one should work. I have mentioned some ideas regarding this topic in earlier chapters. If we are going to rely on the instruction book God left for us, then we have to apply common sense. God said take one day off and work six. Okay, do we really need a thousand-dollar seminar to understand that? Hard work as a means to success is cited over and over in the *Good Book*. However, you must decide on the definition of "hard work." That is a personal choice.

Some people write for 80 hours a week and some people lift bricks for 50 hours a week. I'd say both efforts are hard. The Bible says we should not wear ourselves out to get riches; it doesn't say we should not ever wear ourselves out. I've based my personal philosophy on two ideas. One I adapted from the

Bible: If you wear yourself out seeking God, then you won't have to wear yourself out seeking anything else.

I got the other idea from Zig Ziglar: "Work like everything depends on you, pray like everything depends on God." There is one more point I think must be understood. We've all heard the words ***don't work hard, work smart***. I think people misinterpret this statement completely. I get the gist of what those words convey, but I think people misunderstand them. I know I did. If you are working smart, then you are likely working with your mind.

You are thinking, studying, researching, planning, organizing and developing systems, infrastructure and leverage. And if you are doing that, then you are working hard, very hard. In fact, mental work may be the hardest work there is. I think some people interpret that expression to mean we aren't supposed to work hard. Nothing could be further from the truth. So what's the best answer to whether we should work hard or smart? Both!

It is also important to do what you feel you should do. Not what Bill Gates does; not what your best friend does. Do what you decide you should do. We know our own threshold for hard work, for endurance, for what feels right at the end of a long day. We know when we've really put in some tough hours the same way we know when we've slacked off and just punched the clock.

In exercise there is a target heart rate. I believe there is one with our work as well. Not everybody is the same, nor are we supposed to be. There are too many variables in each individual's life to achieve similarity among us all.

Maybe you see somebody pouring it on at a pace you can't keep up with. Maybe it makes you feel guilty and uneasy. After all, you feel you have been working hard yourself. Don't let that affect you. Maybe while burning the midnight oil every night, that person is neglecting his or her family, spiritual life or health. Maybe that person has slacked off for the last 10 years and just now has to turn it on to catch up. You don't know the whole story of that person's life; only yours. March to your own drum and you will make the best music.

"Half our life is spent trying to find something to do with the time we have rushed through life trying to save."
~ **Will Rogers**

If You Put the Cart Before the Horse, You Might Get Kicked

A few months ago I had breakfast with one of my best friends, Jack. He also happens to be one of my greatest spiritual mentors and the founder of MENSHARPENERS (www.mensharpeners. org), a ministry designed to empower, encourage, support and, you guessed it, sharpen Christian men.

Jack told me about his vision to take his incredible ministry to a much larger, perhaps national, level. Jack was excited *and* confused about where to start. He was trying to figure out what it would look like in five years. He analyzed where to start and how to finish. He pondered over details that didn't yet exist. I definitely believe in writing down long-range dreams and goals. However, I have also seen my life take drastic turns that were completely out of my control, nowhere on my agenda and certainly not programmed in my GPS.

Therefore I learned to focus the most on the next 12 months instead of the next five years. Anyway, I want to share what Jack and I discussed. I think it is an important area that many success-oriented individuals struggle with.

What I am talking about is "sequence." I once had some very demanding clients who pressed me for deadlines every month. I was excellent at meeting those deadlines and extremely creative in the middle of a crisis. Clients asked me all the time, "What are we going to do if ABC happens?" Or, "What if XYX goes wrong?"

Every time I replied with the following metaphor: I told them I didn't worry about what play to call on fourth down until I got to the fourth down. I might score on the second down and never have to deal with it. Or I might be able to kick a field goal. I explained that if I did end up on fourth down, the play I would run would depend on several factors: Where was I on the field? How much time was on the clock? What were the weather conditions? Who's on my team?

The lesson here is that people spend so much time worrying about fourth down that they don't execute the other downs very well. Ironically, if they'll focus on the down they're on, they might score quicker and never end up in fourth down situations. This relates closely to what we have covered about living in the present, but it isn't quite the same thing. Living in the present means being fully conscious about where you are and what you are doing.

And sequence? Sequence is about exercising that consciousness in the most effective and appropriate order. Let's see what Solomon said in Proverbs 24:27, "Finish your outdoor work and get your fields ready, after that build your house." The lesson here is that we should prioritize all aspects of life in their proper order, or **sequence**. If an entrepreneur buys personal things with early profits from the business and doesn't save or reinvest appropriately, then when he faces struggles he may lose both the business and the things he bought. I see commissioned sales people do this all the time.

They go into debt before they become established and end up leaving to get a salaried job. Consequently, they leave what might be an incredible long-term opportunity because they were not in sequence. Too often we see failure as a statement about our intelligence, ingenuity or even our personality. However, failure is more often connected to disciplined sequence and often as simple as not having enough resources in place during that "tipping point" between success and failure. Where did the resources go? Maybe they went to those non-prioritized, non-sequential luxuries.

One of my mentors put me in my place when it came to sequencing. It was about 16 years ago and I was talking about owning a private jet and driving a Lamborghini and just going on and on about how I was going to be a multimillionaire with all this "stuff." He stopped and stared at me for a minute and said, "That's great, Kevin. But if you really want to be a millionaire, you better figure out how to be a thousandaire first." I got his point and from that day on I have always paid attention to **sequence**.

When the Going Gets Tough, the Tough Recall WHY They're Going

In this book I have labored to make clear what I consider to be the most fundamental and yet essential principles for achieving your goals, dreams and purposes for your life. Despite everything I have shared here, I believe there is one particular principle that, if completely understood and capitalized on, could be the only one you need. And that is to have a powerful reason WHY you want to accomplish something?

Winston Churchill said: "Courage is the first of the human qualities because it is the quality which guarantees all the others." I believe your "WHY" is similarly important because it will guarantee you do whatever it takes.

When I look back at my earliest significant success, I realize my reason for attaining it and the meaning attached to attaining it gave me my true power. When I was in high school, all I thought about was winning a state wrestling title. But it was *why* I wanted to win it that drove me the most. I linked winning a state title to many things.

Here are just a few: I would get a college scholarship; I would be popular; I would get a good job because of the accomplishment; I would attract friends as well as the wife of my dreams, which I did, even though she didn't care one lick about wrestling!

Ultimately, I thought I'd end up rich and famous and have the life of my dreams if I could just win the state title. Well, let me tell you, when I was on the wrestling mat, I looked at my opponents like they were trying to take all that stuff away. At that point they weren't just wrestling me. They were wrestling my future and everything I believed was attached to it. I was undefeated my senior year and even though I did not win that state title due to a season-ending injury, it ended up serving me even better. The real lesson here is that if you go to work on your *why*, your why will go to work on you.

Most people just spend a few minutes thinking about what they want and even less time thinking about why they want it. I think you need to spend hours or days on this – until it is buried in your subconscious mind. Think about it until you are unshakably certain; until it doesn't matter what anybody says or what happens around you.

Think about it until you have the attitude depicted in a poster Lou Holtz mentions in his incredible book, *Winning Every Day.* The poster shows a buzzard sitting on a tree limb with a caption below that reads, "Patience, my ass. I'm going to kill somebody!" When your why is as committed as that buzzard, you are on your way.

I believe the strength of your persistence will correspond to the strength of your why and that is why (no pun intended) you need to be clear about what it is. The new "why" I adopted after my wrestling career was over consisted of many different things. It had much more to do with my professional life and why I wanted to succeed. To start, I despised the idea of *having* to work when I was in my 60s and 70s. I saw elderly men and women working during the holidays at grocery stores. I thought, "I don't ever want that to be me. I don't ever want to be in marginal health at 70 years old and have to get up out of bed to work at a grocery store. Especially when it's cold, rainy and my family is getting together for the holidays. I also don't ever want to go through the want ads in my 70s."

Just that thought (and other related thoughts) caused me to work on my skills so I would never be in that position. Robert Kiyosaki also inspired me to modify my why. In his book, *Retire Young, Retire Rich,* he talks about his "why."

I encourage you to read it yourself to get the full details, because that book inspired me to change my "why" again. I set a goal of financial independence for one major reason: to start life over. I thought if I could be financially independent at a young enough age to embark upon a new career, to pursue what I really wanted, to find out who I really was, to explore my spiritual life at the deepest level, then nothing could be better.

Are You Driving in Reverse?

Most of you are probably familiar with the philosophy: **Be, Do, Have**. If not, it simply means that you have to *be* before you can *do* and you must *do* before you can *have*. The problem is most of us get immersed in the doing and the having and neglect the being. We get our thinking in reverse and consequently our results wind up backwards as well.

I have heard of this principle many times but it wasn't until I spent a weekend with Blair Singer (author of *Sales Dogs* and *Little Voice Mastery*) and Jayne Johnson in her Goals Workshop, www.theclearingsight.com, that it really sank in. (If you ever have a chance to attend Jayne's Goals Workshop DO NOT miss it.) When I went to the seminar, I was on a quest to learn how to "do" the things I needed to achieve a higher level of success. I sat in the front row with my notebook open, pen ready and my mind alert. I was just waiting for the instructions on what to "do" next. Part of this eagerness came from my long-held philosophy that said: If you want what somebody's got, do what they do, and you can have what they have. Good advice, but not complete. What I ultimately walked away with was the realization that I had always focused so much on how to do something that I didn't pay the appropriate attention to how to be something. "Doing" certainly has its place, but "being" is the foundation on which it's done.

This is evidenced most noticeably with celebrities, professional athletes and lottery winners. And it's usually because they experience fast external success. As a result of this "overnight success," their external world races past them and they don't know how to manage it. Their *having* outruns their *being*, and they don't know how to cope.

Their subconscious minds go to work to self-correct the problem, which is why we see people in these situations fall into financial problems even when they've had millions of dollars in the past. If the subconscious can't self-correct fast enough, then these people turn to drugs, food, alcohol or whatever it takes to change their state of mind and help them deal with the misalignment of their having and being. Jim Rohn said it best, "If you inherit a million dollars, you better hurry up and become a millionaire."

Let me give you another example. Imagine you get to host the Oprah Winfrey show for a week. The producers are going to give you the entire script in advance and you'll say exactly what Oprah would say. Now, even though you'll be "doing" the exact same thing, do you think you will have the same result? I doubt it.

What's the difference? It's who Oprah "is" and who she has become.

It is not Oprah's doing that has made her progressively more significant nearly as much as it is who she has become. Many talk shows fail. Their format is cut and dried. They have a guest on the show; there is a story and usually an interview. Anyone could "do" a talk show. But not everyone pays the price to "be" the kind of person who can do it. Oprah's charisma, character, likeability and a host of other attributes are the difference between Oprah and someone who only focuses on the doing.

Okay, so maybe Oprah is an extreme example and you can't quite relate. Let me give you a story that should hit closer to home, especially if you are a guy. One of my best friends, Mike, was on a serious mission to be in a relationship and marry again. He had lost his previous wife to cancer and yearned for companionship in his life.

One morning he shared an answer he had received to his persistent prayer request for a wife. He said he was sitting quietly and practically heard God tell him, "If you think I am going to release one of my angels to you the way you behave right now then you have another thing coming." Mike got the point and realized he needed to clean up his act in a few areas and work on his "being" before his prayer would be answered. Mike was focused on the having; God was focused on the being. Now, let's fast forward. Mike paid attention because you should see his wife, Charlotte. She really *is* an angel. She is beautiful on the inside and out and much too beautiful for Mike! In fact, I told Mike that having Charlotte as his wife is about as much proof I would ever need to believe in God!

Most people focus on the doing and having because it is the most tangible thing they see. But remember, we begin the creation process in our mind, with our thoughts, which is our intangible side. Our being works the same way, and when we focus on our being, the doing and the having will fall in place.

We are Human Beings, Not Human Doings

Success and achievement and the manifestation of our goals require all three of the *being, doing* and *having*. The doing and the having are pretty easy for most of us. We can make phone calls, go on sales calls, make plans, check emails and send out proposals. It's the being that we sometimes neglect and put on the back burner. My best advice for improving your being is to do what you have already been doing, but just do more.

For instance, if you read five books a year, start reading 10. If you go to one seminar a year, go to a few more. Read books about people you'd want to be like. Think about yourself in terms of how you would walk, talk and behave when you become the person you want to be. This whole "being" idea is a collaborative effort between your conscious mind, the universe, God, your subconscious mind and all the actions you take.

It is not a magic bullet or a simple prescription, but there *is* a formula. Just keep studying and you will keep becoming. What helped me a lot over the years was to make a list. We all make to-do lists. It's normal to see what needs to be done. Well, if we need to keep reminding ourselves about what to do, doesn't it make sense to remind ourselves about what and how to be?

So instead of writing down a list of goals, instead I write at the top of my to-do list things like, "be patient," "be confident," "be loving," "be present," or "How would you act if you were the best salesperson, etc., in your industry?" Maybe you're a lot smarter than I am, but I need reminding. I have told my wife to remind me when I am not being present with her and the kids. Like when I am holding them in one arm and my iPhone or TV remote in the other. Not surprisingly, she is happy to do it.

The bottom line is that we are habitual. The best way to change habits of *being* is to do them often. The only way to do them often is to remind ourselves. To prove my point, try a silly exercise tomorrow. Just try it for one day. Relocate the trash can in your home or office. Really, do this. Move it to a completely different area. Now, notice how many times you head toward the old place you had the trash can.

If this happens in our physical world, where we can be very clear that we moved the trash can and we even know where we put it, how much more do you think we struggle with this in our intangible habits of thought, especially when it relates to our being?

The importance of *being* came full circle for me one day when I was talking to a group of friends at a men's retreat. In the group was an architect, an engineer, an electrician, a rocket scientist (really) and a contractor. Anyway, I started asking them questions about construction. I learned that usually it takes as long to plan a building project as it does to actually build it. For instance, it may take a year to locate the land, get building permits, secure financing, hire contractors, develop blueprints and then it would take about a year to complete the construction.

What I learned as a result of that story was that the being is about half of the doing and many times it's more. It made me feel a lot better about all the time I spend studying and all the seminars I attend when it seems like life in the outside world is kind of standing still. It's good to know the actual outside/ tangible result will always follow.

Is a Picture *Really* Worth a Thousand Words?

I want to close this chapter by revealing what I think has had more of a positive impact in my life than any other single activity when compared to the amount of time spent on it. These ideas are not new, but I bet some of my perspectives are. I am going to talk a little about visualization in this section, but that's not all. Please do not skip this paragraph because you think you already know about visualization. The fact that you can see with your eyes shut should be enough evidence to take visualization very seriously.

I would like you to imagine starting a fire (and not in your gas fireplace!). Instead, imagine you need to start a basic campground fire. Now imagine having 12 pieces of small wood (known as kindling) that you will light first. However, imagine those 12 pieces are spread all over the place and not even two of them are touching each other. How much good would it do to light even one at this point? After all, it would just burn up – or burn out.

Only when the 12 pieces of kindling are placed together and set on fire could they be effective at their larger mission of starting a fire. Well, your thought life works much the same way. You are a success-oriented individual. You have lots of positive thoughts stored in your head. However, when you wake each day you must start a new fire. When you rise each morning, your thoughts can shift around pretty easily and if you don't gather them and light them on fire shortly after you wake up, then you may not get the chance to start the fire that could heat things up for the whole day.

Have you ever noticed that once you do start a fire it is not easy to put out? You can even dump a bucket of water on it and sometimes it still won't go out. It may die down a bit, but it will fight right back. I have had campfires that didn't go out even when it had been raining for a while. Now, hopefully the parallel I'm drawing here is becoming clear.

VQ-10, or Vision Quest: 10 Minutes

Let me explain how to use this idea. You can call this process what you want. I call it VQ-10 (the VQ means "Vision Quest" and the 10 means "Ten Minutes"). To me, VQ-10 simply means that I am going to deliberately and consciously think about and visualize my goals, plans, who I am and who I will be for 10 minutes.

Let me break it down for you this way:

Vision Quest:

I don't believe there is one specific formula for doing this. But I do believe it is critical to do it. When starting your own version of a VQ-10, do what works for you. As in warming up for physical activity, there are many options. You can jump rope, do jumping jacks, yoga or stretches.

The same holds true in mental warm-ups. You can do affirmations, quote a scripture, visualize, meditate, pray, read, sit still, walk quietly or even do a combination of several things. I came up with Vision Quest from the movie after the same name. It was about a wrestler who decided upon a big goal and worked extremely hard to achieve it. I got in the habit of calling my time of thinking about my goals and my self-ideal as my Vision Quest time.

Ten Minutes:

While format is optional, in this case timing is everything. So the important thing is to spend some time first thing in the morning and organize your thought energy (here is where the "10" of VQ-10 comes in). Additionally I think if you know *why* you are doing it, then you are more likely to do it. When you think of your purpose, your desired destinations and goals, your self-image, your positive attitude and you see yourself performing with excellence you are recording on the DVD (conscious mind) we talked about in Chapter 3. Your subconscious will then begin to play what was recorded and you will experience it as your reality.

Remember, your thoughts are sources of energy.

You are sending out energy to and through your subconscious mind, God, the universe and activating methods beyond our comprehension. You are, in fact, engineering your thoughts and organizing them to become things. They have creative power and they can transcend time and space. The spirit of the universe keeps hearts beating all over the world and it's why when you think of someone you haven't talked to in a long time, out of the blue, the person suddenly calls you.

By bringing the kindling of your thoughts together you give them power. Just like we control our cars by holding the steering wheel, we control our minds by holding our thoughts. When we hold the wheel of thought and keep our eyes on our destination we not only get there, we get there faster and safer. Never think that taking time to visualize or think about your goals in a quiet and relaxed manner is a waste of time. Never think it is magic either. You don't visualize so things will go "poof" into existence. Personally that has never happened for me. If you figure out how to do that please let me know! You do visualize, however, so you can quiet your mind and access wisdom that can only come from silence. You do it so you activate the subconscious on a higher level and receive the most important thing of all – ideas. You need those ideas to create what you are visualizing. Lastly, visualizing is not a passive form of entertainment; it is active work on your goals.

Too Busy NOT to Pray

Let me offer a final perspective that deals with prayer. Martin Luther said: "Tomorrow I plan to work, work, from early until late. In fact I have so much to do that I shall spend the first three hours in prayer."

Now I realize 3 hours is not very practical for most of us. In fact I have been guilty of neglecting this very thing I am talking about. Some days I am lucky to spend 20 minutes in quote unquote "prayer" but hopefully you get my point. Prayer is not always easy, and maybe that's why it's so effective. Anyway, in a time of struggle I was asking God for answers to problems, money for stuff and insight on decisions I needed, and I wanted it quick. The analogy I got back was this: You want DSL speed and you have a dial-up connection.

In other words, the more consistent we are about spending quiet time in whatever manner we see fit, the more consistent and effective we shall surely be at receiving what we need when we need it. I love what Pearl S Buck said: "I love people. I love my family, my children... but inside myself is a place where I live all alone and that's where you renew your springs that never dry up."

Review

- The best way to get where you're going is to be where you are.

- Since driving is 99% of the trip, we better get good at it.

- Learn to place more value in the journey to your goals rather than the accomplishment of them.

- If you're not happy where you are, you won't be happy somewhere else.

- If you don't live in the moment, when will you live?

- Living in the present allows you to accomplish more, not less and with better quality, not worse.

- When we begin to make swift progress toward our goals, we make swift progress toward our obstacles as well.

- Don't choose between working hard or smart. Choose both.

- Are you in sequence?

- What is your why and how strong is it?

- Are you more focused on being, doing or having?

- You can't download with DSL speed if you've got a dial-up connection.

9

ARRIVE

"If we are always arriving and departing, it is also true that we are eternally anchored. One's destination is never a place but rather a new way of looking at things."
~ Henry Miller

The last step in the Success Compass is *Arriving*. After all, once we program our destination and begin driving to our goal, we should logically arrive at the place we intended to go. Every trip has a destination, a point of arrival, but is our journey ever really over?

The Law of Attraction has no expiration date; it works throughout our lives, in good times and bad. Likewise, our journeys are continual, although we regularly categorize and limit them with this destination or that. In college we have a clear "cap" on how long we should stay in school; in business we often have specific parameters for how long we'll stay in this job, this department or even this company.

When it comes to arriving, however, it is important to put it in the context of our life's ongoing journey, not this specific goal or that. People who think they are "finished," really are; they never move on, progress or truly succeed.

Ask any successful business person and he or she will tell you that progress is measured in increments, not plateaus. Success in business and in life is measured by the progress you make in reaching multiple destinations, not just one or two. By the same token, it is important to both appreciate your arrival at one destination while simultaneously programming where you want to go on your next trip.

That's why GPS devices aren't disposable; they are designed to be used over and over again, much as our best life lessons are learned from the experience gained on the way to our destinations, rather than when we get there.

"The road leading to a goal does not separate you from the destination; it is essentially a part of it."
~ Charles DeLint

At face value, this last step in the Success Compass seems pretty simple. As I've already stated, you **program**, you **drive** and then you **arrive**. However, if it's that simple, then why don't we reach our goals every time? After all, when we set out to accomplish our goals, we're usually excited. We realize we don't yet have what we desire, but we're happy and excited at the thought of achieving it. Then, too, we are often just as jazzed about the journey. We truly realize and believe that we create with our thoughts and so we become more conscious of how we use our words and what we think about.

We anticipate the achievement and manifestation of what we desire. We begin taking action and moving toward our goal. And then, little by little, we find ourselves still traveling on this seemingly never-ending road. We wonder if we took a wrong turn. We wonder if it's really what we were meant to do. We question our ability and ultimately come to a fork in the road.

Do we keep persevering and risk losing more than we already have? Or do we cut our losses and say it "just wasn't meant to be"? We wonder if we are being foolish by believing and trusting in the destination we programmed.

Somewhere along the way we do more than lose momentum; we lose our faith.

If You Want Faith, Prepare for Doubt

The most important aspect of arriving, in my opinion and experience, is the easy to define, hard to exercise, word called faith. Faith, of course, is the opposite of doubt (or fear). It is not a physical roadblock that will keep us from our goal nearly as much as a mental one. What we have covered in this book has equipped you with new skills and strategies to strengthen your beliefs. It's been said that if you want peace, prepare for war. Well, I'm telling you that if you want faith, prepare for doubt. And that's what most people fail to do.

Be different than most people; prepare for doubt. Understand that a little doubt isn't just natural, but perfectly healthy. In fact, you should give the enemy of doubt its proper respect. Realize it exists; it *will* attack and you need to have strategies to deal with it.

In this era of salvation through self-help, blended philosophies and a mixing of religions, many of us are taught to deny our feelings, cancel them entirely, change our vibrations or reroute from the negative to the positive – without any realization that pain, suffering, tragedy, toil and, yes, doubt are actually supposed to be a part of our daily lives. (Although, hopefully, not too big of a part.)

We cannot just "think ourselves thin" or "be happy for no reason" without first addressing how to deal with our heavier, unhappier selves. Happiness is a worthy destination, but how can we fully appreciate happiness without understanding what it means to be unhappy?

In this case, ignorance is far from bliss! It is by not preparing for doubt, or even recognizing this enemy in the first place, that one is more likely to fall prey to it. In the literal sense, the only thing that would prevent you from arriving at a physical destination would be if you were to suddenly stop driving. Figuratively speaking, the only thing that will prevent you from arriving at any of your desired destinations will be if you stop believing.

Are You Only Using the First Stage of Your Rocket?

Scripturally speaking, I think Galatians 3:3 offers a sound perspective on how we sabotage our own efforts and fall victim to doubts and fears. Take a look at this short sentence and then let's talk about it: "Are you so foolish? After beginning with the Spirit, are you now trying to attain your goal by human effort?"

Now, of course, this scripture is not talking about goal setting and the Law of Attraction, but I certainly believe we can see how it parallels what we encounter on the journey toward our goals.

So what am I talking about and how does all this tie together? I think it's best illustrated by some additional words from Fred Smith. He said, "Life is a two-stage rocket. The first is physical energy — it ignites and we are off. As physical energy diminishes, the spiritual stage must ignite to boost us into orbit or we fall back and plateau."

Unfortunately, most of us only use one stage — the first stage — of our rockets.

When we begin the journey toward our goals, we desperately want to believe their achievement is possible. We believe in the Law of Attraction and how the universal spirit will coordinate details beyond our comprehension to help us achieve our desired results. But somewhere along the way, we abandon the course in which we had the courage to pursue in the first place. Maybe it's taking too long, maybe we have encountered excessive adversity and things are unfolding completely different than we expected... or maybe we can't maintain belief.

Whatever the reason, you must trust that the course you are on will serve your best interests if you will only keep your eyes open, marshal your energy and let the second stage of your personal rocket kick in.

When you program a GPS, it becomes sort of like a Terminator, aiming toward the destination. It doesn't care how many times you screw up, take a wrong turn or stop to stretch your legs. It will keep recalculating until you either make the correct turns or abandon the trip altogether, delete the destination and start over with a new one.

If there are detours and obstacles far ahead (and only the GPS can see them that far down the road), you don't want to question the environment and circumstances you are in before you get there. Maybe you are supposed to get a flat tire (metaphorically or literally) so you will be in a certain place to meet a certain person at a certain time.

Questions are useful, but the time to ask them is before you start the journey, not miles and miles down the road. If you are going to start out trusting, then you need to finish up trusting. The main reason people don't finish what they set out to do is not because they quit working, it's because they quit believing. It will require belief to begin a journey and it will require even more belief to finish it.

And if you don't *finish* believing, believe me, *you are finished*.

"Every happening, great and small is a parable whereby God speaks to us, and the art of life is to get the message."
~ Malcolm Muggeridge

"Paint the Fence!"

There are many techniques to help strengthen our faith and belief, and we learned several in earlier chapters. If you recall, I believe God speaks to me through analogies and pictures I receive when I am sitting quietly and doing my best to think about nothing.

Well, He did it again. One day I was particularly frustrated about my journey. I was having challenges with employees, sales were down and a host of other problems made my particular career choice highly suspect. Furthermore, I wasn't really doing what I wanted to be doing within my own company.

I had different dreams and goals and didn't understand how they fit into the bigger picture. I was asking God for a change. I was reminded of a movie, and as always, God didn't deliver me from my circumstances, but instead He showed me a different way to look at them. In the movie "The Karate Kid," Mr. Miyagi (played by Noriyuki "Pat" Morita) agrees to teach a young boy, Daniel, who he calls "Daniel-son," karate if he will do some work for him at his home. Before Daniel-son gets any lessons, Mr. Miyagi has him paint the fence, wax the car and sand his deck.

It was hard work. Finally, Daniel-son gets worn out and gets so frustrated he confronts Mr. Miyagi. He begins to complain and argue that the old man is not holding up his end of the deal. Mr. Miyagi then demonstrates how all the movements that Daniel-son is making with his painting, sanding and waxing are preparing him perfectly for his desired goal of learning karate. Mr. Miyagi begins to swing and strike at Daniel-son, but before he does, he says, "Paint the fence." Daniel-son then begins to emulate the same movements he did when he was painting the fence.

This demonstration continues and picks up speed and intensity, and finally Daniel-son has the message. Hopefully, the lesson is as clear for you as well. If not, go rent the movie! I don't believe we are anywhere by accident. Whenever you are in circumstances that are unpleasant, confusing or frustrating, just trust that your Teacher is working for your good. Our

Teacher knows we need the process as much, if not more, than the finished product. What fences are you complaining about painting that are for your own good?

Realize that even though you may be paying your dues, stuck in a cubicle, toiling away in corporate bureaucracy, the call-center or even painting a fence, there *is* a plan and "someone" out there knows what it is. Even if you can't see your destination through all the fog, rain, wind, sleet or dust, **know** you are on the right path and trust the journey to reveal your desired destination, or something better.

"Paint the fence!"

Rejoice in Trials... Are You Nuts?

"Consider it pure joy, my brothers, whenever you face trials of many kinds, because you know that the testing of your faith develops perseverance. Perseverance must finish its work so that you may be mature and complete, not lacking anything. If any of you lacks wisdom, he should ask God, who gives generously to all without finding fault, and it will be given to him. But when he asks, he must believe and not doubt, because he who doubts is like a wave of the sea, blown and tossed by the wind. That man should not think he will receive anything from the Lord. He is a double minded man, unstable in all he does." James 1:1-8

It would probably be a good idea to read the preceding paragraph about 10 times. It sums up a lot of what we've been talking about. It doesn't just tell us what perspective to have about adversity. It also tells us *we must believe* and *not doubt*.

If you master and apply nothing more than the words in that paragraph, you will reach high stations in life. Belief in yourself and your journey is the key to getting where you want to go.

Doubt kills progress. By inviting it and/or not evicting it, you will rarely arrive where you want to go, let alone where you were meant to be. Oswald Chambers, a prominent twentieth-century minister and teacher best known for his popular devotional, *My Utmost for His Highest,* said, "God will never reveal more truth about Himself till you obey what you already know." So literally, the more you doubt the less you know – and the less you know the less you shall know.

How Fast is Your Mental Metabolism?

If you participate in regular exercise, let me ask you a question. Why do you do it? I am sure there are lots of reasons but the foundation of all the benefits exercise offers is being at an ideal weight. Most of us work-out and exercise so we can stay in good physical shape, increase our metabolism and keep body fat at bay.

So my next question for you is, "How fast is your *mental* metabolism?" "How quickly can you burn up the negative mental calories you consume from your plate of life?"

And what can we do to speed up the process?

This isn't the same as learning 10 vocabulary words a day to get smarter or build a bigger brain. This is learning to recognize the difference between positive thoughts (calories) and negative, or junk, thoughts (calories).

When you do resistance training, i.e. lift weights, you build more muscle. The great thing about building muscle is that it kicks up your metabolism to help burn off calories faster. With that thinking, we can logically assume the more positive thoughts you "ingest," the more positive you'll feel about life, yourself, your journey and your destination. Likewise, the quicker and easier it is to digest and get rid of those negative thoughts throughout the day.

We Don't "Arrive" Until Doubt "Departs"

We've already learned that doubt derails our journey through life, often before it even begins. Think about how many times you've been inspired to reach some goal, get someplace or do something – and I mean really, really jazzed about it – only to let that negative junk food imply you're "not good enough," "not smart enough" or "not ready" to get there. One of the best ways to conquer doubt is to believe that "all things work together for good" and that what you want (or something even better) is on its way.

The Most Pain Comes Right Before Delivery!

Apparently it's a little bit uncomfortable when a woman gives birth. I don't see what all the fuss is about, but let's assume it's true for the sake of my example ☺. From what I have heard and seen on TV, it appears the most pain comes on the last push. It is the final grunt and screams that precede the birth. I think the journey to any of our goals and destinations is very similar. We are in labor for a long time and it is gets to be very uncomfortable. We are tired, emotional and simply ready to "arrive" and be done with our current trip.

If we're not careful, it is easy to misinterpret the pain we are going through. I personally have experienced pain I thought was going to kill me, when in fact it was the final push I needed to give birth to a goal. We must always remember that whatever we programmed is what will arrive. By forgetting this basic principle, we will buy into fear and doubt when we should instead hold on for dear life and accept the final pains of labor that deliver our miracle.

Remember, *it's not all up to you*; unseen hands are guiding your journey, providing guardrails even when you think you're too far off course to stay on the road. Strong faith in these supernatural guardrails will erase doubt when it threatens to derail your entire journey.

As you grow from a caterpillar to a butterfly, there will be a time when you aren't either one. You will be wrapped in a cocoon of confusion and doubt and you may feel weak, vulnerable, helpless and hopeless. But, like anyone – or anything – that experiences a true metamorphosis or change, this is a process you have to experience **before you can fly**.

Recognizing that life often works this way will help you stay strong in your faith. It will serve as a much needed reminder that you are in a process which will allow you to fly higher. It will give you the faith to know that you're not in a dark time that will be the end of you, but rather a dark time that is preparing you to fly. In your life you will most certainly have times of trouble and you'll get into some doubt and disbelief. The key, however, is to never let doubt and disbelief get into *you*.

Believing big is not the problem for most people; it's believing consistently that is challenging. We're all taught to think outside the box, dream big and then dream even bigger! Most people need to "see it to believe it," but faith means we need to *believe it before we can see it*.

Be patient and trust in the journey. Remember, Jesus spent 30 years in a carpenter's shop before He was promoted to His ultimate purpose. If the man who had the *biggest mission in the world* spent 30 years in a carpenter's shop, just maybe the "shop" you're in could be preparing you for something greater as well.

If Life Isn't About Process, We Would Be Born As Adults

Let's not get confused about this whole "Arriving" deal. It is okay to arrive; it's important to get there. Every goal we achieve puts doubt in its place and dares it to rear its ugly head again! And, yes, we *should* absolutely celebrate the destinations we reach without feeling the best part of the journey is behind us.

The point I am trying to illustrate (which is easy to illustrate but much harder to live) is we must flip-flop our value of the driving versus the destination. We have looked at it in many ways throughout this book, and I hope it's sinking in by now. We have to believe the journey isn't just a means to an end, but an end-all unto itself.

I've found another way to look at this. My wife and I had a goal to have children. When our first baby was born, that could certainly have been labeled a destination, an arrival. However, we then had to raise this little baby. I think goals are pretty much the same. We **program** what we want, we **drive** to it, we **arrive** and *then* we begin raising what we birthed. Have a big family – a big family of goals, of destinations, of hopes, of dreams, of achievements and arrivals! Giving birth is a destination, but then we raise the child. You will spend your life raising your goals. And you can have as big a family as you want!

His Ways ARE Higher Than Our Ways

I was extremely excited about the possibility of Kurt Warner of the Arizona Cardinals winning Super Bowl XLIII in 2009. I was sure God would allow it to happen. It didn't matter to me what teams were playing that year; I was just rooting for Kurt and the Cinderella story I knew he would write. I respected both the Arizona Cardinals and the Pittsburg Steelers for reaching the Super Bowl and each had outstanding players, but this was Kurt's year and that's all I could focus on. Well, despite a valiant effort in a very exciting and nail biting game, Kurt Warner did *not* get the victory in that Super Bowl.

I was bummed out. A few days later, I was talking to my friend Paul and said, "Doesn't it confuse you as to why God wouldn't take advantage of an awesome opportunity to glorify His name, knowing Kurt always gives Him the credit? God could have caused them to win the Super Bowl!"

Paul said, "I think He *did* take advantage of it. To begin, God is much more concerned about our character development than our accomplishments. He is more concerned about what we possess on the inside than the outside."

Then Paul offered a perspective I'd missed. He said, "Did you see the post-game interviews with Kurt?"

I said, "Yeah, why?"

He said, "If you didn't know the outcome of the game before you started watching, you might have not been clear from watching Kurt. He was upbeat, his head was held high and he was very positive." Paul reminded me of something I tend to forget, "If you falter in times of trouble, how small is your strength."

Ultimately, Paul said, God *did* take advantage of an opportunity to be glorified. It's widely known that Kurt Warner is a Christian. By conducting himself as he did, before, during and after what must be one of the greatest roller coaster rides in sports (the pre-game hype, then losing the championship game, especially as close as they came) Kurt Warner demonstrated a Christian's walk in faith more than if they'd won.

In our shallow thinking, we tend to measure success and blessings by what shows up on the outside. But by remembering that our essence is spiritual and intangible, it shouldn't surprise us that the greatest growth and accomplishment we can experience is more spiritual anyway. This was a good lesson for me. It doesn't change the fact that I still want Kurt to win a Super Bowl again one day, but maybe I will handle it better if he doesn't!

Laughing Over Spilled Milk

Ten years ago, I received a Mont Blanc pen as a gift. I use it almost every day and guard it with my life. However, a few years ago I obviously wasn't guarding it that well because it went missing for more than two months.

I looked everywhere at my home and office. I finally reconciled to the fact I had lost it forever. Then, one night I was giving my daughter a bottle of milk as we sat in her rocker chair. The cap on the milk hadn't been attached correctly (probably my wife's fault!) and milk spilled all over me, my daughter and the chair. We both yelled... ahhhhhh!

My wife stormed in to see what all the fuss was about. I picked up my daughter and went to the bathroom to clean her up. In the meantime, my wife pulled the cushion off of the rocker to clean up the milk and lo and behold, there was my pen! Now, the lesson here isn't to start spilling milk any time you lose something, get disappointed or hit a roadblock; the lesson is you just never know how things are going to turn out!

As we close this chapter I must say that the struggle between faith and doubt will never end. Fortunately, neither will our ability to win those struggles. I hope you enjoyed, learned and grew in our journey together. I leave you not with all the answers, but with the wisdom that you must never stop asking questions. Success will ultimately go to the askers, the seekers and the knockers. Be true to your self and don't be fooled. And as Theodore Rubin said; "There are two ways to slide easily through life: to believe everything or to doubt everything; both ways save us from thinking."

I appreciate your commitment to finishing this book. I hope you have gleaned new insight and perspectives that will help you along in your journeys. I encourage you to visit my website, **www.TheSuccessCompass.com**, and I would love to meet you at one of our workshops.

As we approach this particular destination together, I would like to challenge you to be true to yourself. You probably have a good idea about what you really want in life and what your purpose should be. It will typically beckon to all of us. The problem is we drown it out with fear, busyness, activities, excuses and procrastination. One of the major premises of this book is to take what isn't and transform it into what is. However, this book can't do that for you. No coach, seminar or anything else can do it either. Only YOU can be the instrument on which the laws of the universe will play.

It is up to you.

Surrender the past, live in the present and behold, you will be, do and have your future. You will program, you will drive, and you will surely arrive.

Review

- If you want faith, prepare for doubt.

- It's not physical roadblocks we need to worry about, but the mental ones.

- You must not only begin believing, you must finish believing.

- Are you complaining about any fences you are painting?

- How fast is your mental metabolism?

- Always believe what you want is "on its way."

- The challenge is not in believing big, but in consistently believing.

All things work for your best...
if you believe they do.

BONUS CHAPTER

For Network Marketers and Salespeople *Only!*

Sales & Recruiting Principles from the Greatest Salesman in the World

Why a special section just for you? As a salesperson, network marketer and/or entrepreneur, you face unique opportunities – and adversities – most people don't. For example, in your field, you have a potential to earn income that is higher than any other field. Unfortunately, you are also susceptible to **more risk**, **more disappointment** and **more loss** than most professions combined. Living with both sides of this entrepreneurial coin, you will likely experience more exhilarating highs and more debilitating lows than any other type of professional venture known to man.

Those of us in this field also tend to have an above average amount of information thrown at them. We get more email, more junk mail, more solicitations, etc. We have to decipher through more legitimate (and illegitimate) information and ideas than the average Joe. We are also exposed to more travel, irregular schedules, sleep deprivation, inconvenient eating habits and inconsistent physical exercise.

As a result of being constantly bombarded with internal and external demands, having faith one day and experiencing doubt the next, I decided to develop a list of "power thoughts" that I could reference to keep me on track (mentally). If you've read this entire book, you know why I use the Bible as a success guide. If you didn't read the book and just skipped to this chapter, then what the heck are you doing!? Go back and read; this chapter will still be here when you're through!

Seriously, though, no matter what your religious or spiritual beliefs, it is undeniable that Jesus created the biggest group of "representatives" in the history of any recruitment effort. He was able to accomplish this without the help of the Internet, brochures, telephones, Blackberries, iPhones or even email (he did host a few seminars though). He also recruited millions with a base of just "12 distributors." Therefore, I thought it would be of some benefit to learn from the **Top Producer of All Time**, especially since He can still out-recruit and out-sell anybody, and He isn't even alive, in a physical sense. After careful examination, I extracted some of Jesus' most profound insights as they relate to selling, recruiting and playing the entrepreneurial game. I put them in a sort of sequence or flow chart to provide a mental blueprint, a track to run on so to speak.

Now, please hear me loud and clear: I am not trying to modify scripture or twist any truths. I am not a victim of misinterpretation. The examples in this chapter are here to help you expand your mind, sharpen your philosophy and improve your results. This is a bonus chapter designed to help you, not stir up a debate about what the Bible really meant. I will paraphrase certain scriptures for the purposes of clarifying the examples. Have some fun and more importantly learn something. I am simply having fun with the parallels I draw and hopefully you can see how they relate.

After careful examination, the "power thoughts" I selected seemed to be the most effective scriptures for this entrepreneurial game. They are simply a sequence of thoughts and principles to keep me on track in my inner world so I can stay on track in my outer world. I developed it because I wanted something I could refer to again and again as I was fighting the battles of daily life. See, I think you need protection and defenses that correspond with the sport you are playing. For example, football players wear all kinds of pads and a helmet. Soccer players (nothing against soccer here) may only wear a pair of knee pads.

We all know business is a "contact sport," so what special equipment do we need? A receptionist may only need a thought that says "this too shall pass." But we will need much more than a warm and fuzzy quote at times. I feel we need a series of thoughts, organized thoughts, that take care of us while we "fight for ass." So here we go. I will outline what I consider to be some of the best thinking we can adopt in our particular field of endeavor and make comments about each one.

Also, I am using the terms "downline, representatives, salespeople, etc" interchangeably. For the most part it means a group of sales people in direct selling. It may be in network marketing and it may not. But it also applies to a single salesperson who is trying to build a client base. If you are selling something (and we all are) you can extract the lessons and apply them to the game you are playing.

I doubt you are in this field (sales, network marketing entrepreneur, etc.) if you don't have high aspirations. I also assume you have a commitment to excellence. Therefore, it is also safe to assume you aspire to greatness, so that is where we will start:

If You Want To Be Great, You Must Be A Servant (Matthew 20: 26-27)

Many people would be far more successful if they paid attention to this verse and nothing else. When you realize that success or greatness in *any* endeavor is a result of service to others, then you will focus on service and success will follow.

Forget about yourself.

Forget about your income.

Focus on getting your valuable product or service into others' hands. Your job is not to reap; your job is only to sow.

Some people insist it's all about results. In truth, of course, it *is* all about results. But, if the service is there, the results will naturally follow. If you're not getting the results you want, then you only need to examine your service.

For the Son of Man came to Seek and Save the Lost
(Luke 19:10)

Your mission is to seek and save the lost of a different kind. The people who are caught in the ignorance of our changing world; caught in Industrial Age thinking while we live in an Information Age, an age that requires a new set of ideas, rationales and responses.

These are the people who resist change due to fear, denial and ignorance; the people who need 'awareness' salvation the most. It's the people who are unaware of the awesome philosophies and thinking strategies available to them.

Your job is to seek out people who are unaware that a book like *Think and Grow Rich* exists. You must rescue those who have not read *Rich Dad, Poor Dad* and, of course you must save those who don't have a copy of *The Success Compass!* You must encourage others to embrace the best teaching so it can embrace them. Look for the people who don't realize that sales (and direct sales) are the wave of the future and offer more opportunity than any other field. They need to know this field doesn't discriminate and doesn't care about your background and education. And you must also realize why you will deal with difficult people at times.

One time Jesus was questioned as to why He was hanging out with certain (substandard) people. His response was, "It is not the healthy who need a doctor, but the sick." You, too, will have to get your hands dirty and filter through the sick, find the lost and show them the way.

Jesus went throughout Galilee, teaching, preaching and healing
(Matt 4:23)

This is related to seek and save the lost. You, too, will need to heal, teach and preach your message. By exposing people to a higher awareness and exposing them to training as well as the products and services you offer, you are *healing* their ignorance, you are *teaching* better thinking and you are *preaching* hope, opportunities and advancement. When you think of yourself only as a sales or marketing person, you miss out on the real mission, the mission of a master who came: to *heal, teach and preach*.

If You Are Faithful With A Few Things, You Will Be Put In Charge of Many
(Matt 25: 14-30)

In Matthew 25: 14-30, we learn the importance of good stewardship with our time, talents and resources, even when the amounts are small. It's like saying, "I will get my finances organized and start saving *as soon as I have some money.*"

No, no, no, no, no – and one more time, NO! Once you get your finances organized and start saving money, then you will have some. Building your business requires the same philosophy.

You don't say, "I will really systemize and pour into my downline when I have lots of people..." If you pour into one person, you will then have many. I started a business more than 10 years ago. When I cultivated my first client, I treated him like he was the only person in the world. Due to my service level, he then referred me out and I built a complete client base through referrals only (no advertising or marketing expense) because of *his* network. And I did it very quickly.

I never have and I never will worry about the amount of anything – be it people, resources, time, or energy – when I set out toward a goal. If I trust in the miracle-working process I have covered in this book, then I will remember how a couple of fish and a few loaves of bread fed thousands.

The Parable of the Sower
(Mark 4:3-8)

Even Jesus knew many would misunderstand and reject his messages. He also knew He needed to keep it simple so He almost always shared His message through parables. He displayed an attribute that would take us to heights and beyond our dreams if we could only adopt it with unwavering commitment. Jesus showed us how important it is **to never give up on your vision and your mission because someone else doesn't believe in it or support it**.

In this parable, we learn about what happens when a farmer went out to sow seed. Jesus explains that as the farmer scattered his seed, some of it fell along the path and the birds came and ate it. Some of the seed fell on rocky places, where there was not much soil. It sprang up quickly because the soil was shallow. But when the sun came up, the plants were scorched and they withered because they had no roots. Other seed fell among thorns, which grew up and choked the plants, so they did not produce grain. Still other seed fell on good soil. It came up, grew and produced a crop, multiplying thirty, sixty or even a hundred times.

I hope the parallel here is clear. As you sow the seed of opportunity, you will encounter different responses. Some people will be too negative and cynical to accept it. They are the seed that the birds eat up. Others will get excited and then get knocked out of the game because one person says something like, "It sounds like a pyramid deal." Still others will get going and have the wrong motives, values and perspectives and lose heart when the going gets tough.

Finally, there will always be those who are ready; those who "get it" and produce a harvest beyond expectations. Jesus did not stop teaching, preaching and healing because of these four very different types of soil. No, He kept going *because of them*.

How about you?

Shake Off Rejection
(Matthew 10:14)

Here is another thought related to the one above. In this example, Jesus tells His "sales team", "If no one welcomes you or listens to your words, as you leave that house or town, shake its dust off your feet." (Matthew 10:14)

Notice what He did not say. He did not say, "If no one welcomes you, then you should quit, get depressed and re-evaluate your entire life." Oh yeah, and what about your friends and family?

Well, the Greatest Distributor covered that one as well. In Matthew 13:57, Jesus says, "Only in his hometown and in his own house is a prophet without honor." Some people thought Jesus was crazy – and some people will think you are, too. So when your best friend from high school thinks you're nuts, don't be surprised at all; you're in good company.

Jesus taught his "sales reps" many things. He taught them about money, success and how to think. He taught them how to prioritize, how to treat others and how to behave. He taught them what to value and the importance of discipline. He also taught much, much more.

However, in an emotional statement I believe He intended to use as a "catch-all" statement to reconcile the good, the bad and the ugly. He said the following words to His team: "I have told you these things, so that in me you may have peace. In this world you will have trouble. But be of good cheer! I have overcome the world." (John 16: 33)

How Network Marketing (Practically) Saved My Life

Despite my conviction about the direct selling industry, I have not been actively involved for many years. However, I feel it is important to share my perspectives because my experience in the industry has had more to do with my growth, awareness, inspiration and motivation than all my collective professional experiences combined. I would not be who I am if I hadn't become involved in direct selling/network marketing. The biggest reason I have not been active for years is because I took what I learned and applied it to other business models and have not had the time.

Despite what some people say, I believe there is no such thing as failure in the direct selling industry. I believe there is no other profession in the world where you have the opportunity to learn as much as you want to learn and become as much as you want to become than you will with network marketing. I think in many instances I would rather spend a year failing in network marketing than four years in school or two years in a high-paying job. With a twist on what Jim Rohn says, I say join network marketing not for what you will get, but **what it will make of you** and **who you will become**.

The people who criticize network marketing companies simply don't understand them. Sure, there are bad companies out there, but there are many more good than bad. We find the same thing in corporate America, don't we? In fact, in more recent times we have probably seen more violations of integrity and legal business practice than we would ever find in the direct selling industry.

Then there are those who say only the people at the top make money. That is not true. When you become a direct sales distributor, you are essentially "on top." You are at the top of your own pyramid. Your job is to fill in the bottom. And here is another good thought, there are enough people who will get involved not to worry about the ones who won't.

There are also enough people in the world to put as many people below you who are already above you. Therefore, the comment that the people on top make all the work money is true, because they *built something underneath*. Now it's your turn! The opposite is found in corporate America, where you start at the bottom and almost never make it to the top.

Despite all I have shared, I've still witnessed more bad, negative and incorrect perspectives about the industry than I would like. Therefore, I would like to offer some different views that I feel are worth considering. These are not from any special survey. They come from what I have witnessed in my own involvement:

The Top Reasons Most People **Join** Network Marketing

- To get rich

- To be their own boss

- To earn extra income

- To be around positive people

- To be a part of something

The Top Reasons Most People **Quit** Network Marketing

- They are not getting rich overnight

- They don't have a good boss

- Not much extra income

- They blame their sponsor for lack of success

They are ignorant of business skills and never learn that network marketing is a business, not a hobby.

When you look at them closely, you'll see that most of these reasons for joining – and quitting – network marketing are unjustified and irrational.

I will not go into great detail here, but I will offer a different perspective: **Getting rich should be the last reason you join anything**. Who you can become and what you can learn should be your first consideration, and how you can contribute to others should be second. If you make those goals your main focus, then you will make different decisions and achieve different results. You will also have a different tolerance for the time you need to create a profitable situation. Everything you learn in direct sales prepares and equips you to handle a bigger plate of responsibility, which is what makes you rich anyway.

Try to look at network marketing as a university or college for entrepreneurship and business skills. Most of us never learned very much about these skill sets in high school or college. To get the opportunity to actually make money and with a small investment in training and possibly some travel, you can learn the skills from very successful people that would otherwise take years and years of trial and error. Besides that, the education you get in network marketing is all relevant. You don't have any basket weaving electives. It will apply to anything that lies in your future, whether it is direct selling or not.

If your goal was to be a doctor, would you drop out of school in your second year because you weren't rich yet? Of course not, but that is exactly what people who quit for that type of reason are doing. They didn't understand why they were getting involved in the first place and, consequently, got out without any understanding.

The truth is, the top of the network marketing system is open to everyone — unlike traditional business systems, which allow only one person to reach the top of the company. Although it sounds exclusive, the way to the top is fairly simple and, more than anything else, requires long-lasting commitment to the mission. The reason most people do not reach the top (which is a subjective statement usually classified in financial terms only) is simply because *they quit too soon*.

Most people join only to make money. If they don't make money in the first few months or years, they become discouraged and quit (and then often bad-mouth the industry). Others quit and look for a company with a better compensation plan. But joining to make a few quick dollars is not the reason to get into the business.

Let me offer a simple statement that summarizes why you should get into network marketing: **the real reason is so the skills of network marketing can get into you**. To exemplify this simple tenet, below is profound story that I think will change your life. I first read it through an email I got from www. richdad.com. Robert Kiyosaki is perhaps the biggest and most effective advocate for teaching people how to transform their financial lives by transforming their thinking. The following story he tells is one of the most transforming I have ever read. Keep reading and see why:

> Once upon a time there was a quaint little village. It was
> a great place to live except for one problem. The village

had no water unless it rained. To solve this problem once and for all, the village elders decided to put out to bid the contract to have water delivered to the village on a daily basis. Two people volunteered to take on the task and the elders awarded the contract to both of them. They felt that a little competition would keep prices low and ensure a back-up supply of water.

Self-Employed Thinking

The first of the two people who won the contract, Ed, immediately ran out, bought two galvanized steel buckets and began running back and forth along the trail to the lake a mile away. He immediately began making money as he labored morning to dusk hauling water from the lake with his two buckets. He would empty them into the large concrete holding tank the village had built. Each morning he had to get up before the rest of the village awoke to make sure there was enough water for the village when it wanted it. It was hard work, but he was very happy to be making money and for having one of the two exclusive contracts for this business.

Business Owner Thinking

The second winning contractor, Bill, disappeared for a while. He was not seen for months, which made Ed very happy since he had no competition. Ed was making all the money.

Instead of buying two buckets to compete with Ed, Bill had written a business plan, created a corporation, found four investors, employed a president to do the work and returned six months later with a construction crew. Within a year his team had built a large-volume stainless steel pipeline which connected the village to the lake. At the grand opening celebration, Bill announced that his water was cleaner than Ed's water. Bill knew that there had been complaints about dirt in Ed's water. Bill also announced that he could supply the village with water 24 hours a day, 7 days a week. Ed could only deliver water on the weekdays; he did not work on weekends. Then Bill announced that he would charge 75% less than Ed did for this higher quality and more reliable source of water. The village cheered and ran immediately for the faucet at the end of Bill's pipeline. In order to compete, Ed immediately lowered his rates by 75%, bought two more buckets, added covers to his buckets and began hauling four buckets each trip. In order to provide better service, he hired his two sons to give him a hand for the night shift and on weekends. When his boys went off to college, he said to them, "Hurry back because someday this business will belong to you." For some reason, after college, his two sons never returned. Eventually

Ed had employees and union problems. The union was demanding higher wages, better benefits and wanted its members to only haul one bucket at a time.

Bill, on the other hand, realized that if this village needed water then other villages must need water, too. He rewrote his business plan and went off to sell his high speed, high volume, and low cost and clean water delivery system to villages throughout the world. He only makes a penny per bucket of water delivered, but he delivers billions of buckets of water, and all that money pours into his bank account. Bill had developed a pipeline to deliver money to himself as well as water to the villages. Bill lived happily ever after and Ed worked hard for the rest of his life and had financial problems forever after.

The end.

That story about Bill and Ed has guided me for years. It has assisted me in my life's decision-making process. I often ask myself, "Am I building a pipeline or hauling buckets?" In fact, the next time someone criticizes you or says you are chasing a "pipe-dream," you can simply respond, "That's exactly what I am doing!"

ABOUT THE AUTHOR

Kevin Hocker is the President of Success Partners Worldwide, a company specializing in human achievement. He is an inspirational business coach, engaging speaker and resilient entrepreneur.

He is also the CEO of Federal Benefits Group, www.federalbenefitsgroup.com, a private company that provides educational and financial services to federal employees. He is the co-author of: *Maximizing Your Federal Benefits, A Government Employee's Survival Guide.*

Kevin's purpose is to help others achieve their goals and dreams by sharing what he's learned through both failure and success as an entrepreneur, sales professional, author and speaker.

Kevin has studied success principles for over 20 years and has been a top producing sales and marketing professional in many different fields. He has successfully designed several business systems, sales processes and marketing plans in the financial services and internet marketing fields.

He has applied much of what he learned as an athlete in competitive wrestling and football to the business world. Kevin believes sports can have a very important role in shaping the character and discipline of young adults and children.

He has a special passion for coaching sales people and first time authors.

Kevin is happily married and has two children.

QUICK ORDER FORM

Fax orders: 314-754-9770. Send this form.

Website orders: www.TheSuccessCompass.com

Please send the following books.

_____ Copies of The Success Compass (19.95)

Name: _____

Address: _____

_____

City: _____ State: _____ Zip: _____

Telephone: _____

Email address: _____

Card Type (circle one):   VISA   MasterCard   AMEX   Discover

Name on Card: _____

Card Number: _____

Exp. Date: _____   Security Code: _____

Signature: _____

The Success Compass – Your Roadmap for Results:

Please send me _____ number of books at $19.95 each.

TOTAL PRICE: _____ US DOLLARS

Sales tax: Please add 7.75% for products shipped to California addresses.

Shipping:

US: $4.00 for first book and $1.00 for each additional book.

International: $11.00 for first book and $6.00 for each additional book.

For quantity discounts, promotions or joint ventures of The Success Compass, please call 877-317-4167.

LET'S CONTINUE OUR JOURNEY

WWW.THESUCCESSCOMPASS.COM

FIND OUT MORE ABOUT:

- Writing your own book
- Live events
- Coaching
- Mastermind Groups

MUCH MORE...

CONTACT THE AUTHOR:

KEVIN HOCKER

ADDRESS: 6209 MID RIVERS MALL DRIVE, SUITE 290
SAINT CHARLES, MO 63304

PHONE: 877-317-4167

EMAIL: KEVIN@THESUCCESSCOMPASS.COM

WEBSITE: WWW.THESUCCESSCOMPASS.COM